The Curious Child's Encyclopedia

101 Why Questions Kids Actually Ask

Claire Monroe

This book belongs to:

Contents

Contents

Introduction

Hello.

You're about to discover something extraordinary. And the answer to almost every question in this book is hiding right under your nose — in your body, your kitchen, your backyard, and the sky above your head.

Right now, your heart is firing an electrical signal without being told to. The sky is scattering blue light in every direction. Somewhere, a jellyfish is still stinging things even though it's dead. And your gut contains more bacteria than there are stars visible from Earth.

None of this is magic. All of it is science. And most of it is far stranger than anything anyone could make up.

This book asks 101 questions — the ones kids actually ask, the ones parents fumble through, and a few that will make everyone at the dinner table stop and stare. Each question gets four things: a quick answer, a deeper explanation, something you can try yourself, and a question that leads somewhere even more interesting.

You don't have to read in order. Start with the grossest one. Follow the "Ask This Next" trail and see where it takes you — question to question, chapter to chapter, right to the edge of what science currently knows.

For the kids: every single fact in here is real. If something sounds too wild to be true, look it up. It is.

For the grown-ups: the science is accurate, the tone is honest, and some of these answers will surprise you just as much as they surprise the children.

101 questions. Eight chapters. No boring answers.
Shall we start with why the sky is blue — or skip straight to the farts?

Claire Monroe

Bonus

Enjoying the Book? Here's a FREE Bonus Just for You!

As a thank-you for reading this far, I've put together an exclusive free bonus gift to help you and your child in their learning journey.

What's Inside the Bonus?

- The Grossest Questions We Didn't Include

Grab your free gift now at:
http://books.bookfunnel.com/curiouschild

You will also be invited for future early book launches with free ebooks being made available.

It's my way of saying thank you. No spam. No fluff. Just value.

Cheers,

Claire Monroe
ChangeLifeReads

Chapter 1

Sky & Space

Have you ever looked up and wondered why the sky is blue, why stars twinkle, or what would actually happen if you took off your spacesuit in space? In this chapter we explore 14 of the biggest questions about everything above our heads — from the atmosphere to the edge of the universe.

In this chapter:

1. Why Is the Sky Blue?
2. Why Does the Sky Turn Red at Sunset?
3. Why Does the Moon Change Shape?
4. Why Do We Have Day and Night?
5. Why Do We Have Seasons?
6. Why Do Stars Twinkle?
7. Why Do Comets Have Tails?
8. Why Do Planets Stay in Orbit?
9. Why Do We Always See the Same Side of the Moon?
10. Why Is the Sun So Much Bigger Than It Looks?
11. Why Do Shooting Stars Streak Across the Sky?
12. ⚡ Why Is Space Black With Billions of Stars?
13. ⚡ Why Would Your Blood Boil in Space?
14. Why Do Astronauts Grow Taller in Space?

#1 Why Is the Sky Blue?

Quick Answer

Sunlight contains all colors. When it hits air, blue light bounces around more than other colors — so blue fills the whole sky when you look up.

Let's Go Deeper

Sunlight looks white but hides a rainbow inside. Tiny air particles scatter blue light in all directions because blue has shorter wavelengths. At sunset the sun is lower, light travels through more air, and blue scatters away — leaving red and orange.

Try It Yourself

Shine a torch through a glass of water mixed with a drop of milk. View from the side — it looks bluish. That's the same scattering as our sky.

Ask This Next

Why does the sky turn red at sunset? → #2

#2 Why Does the Sky Turn Red at Sunset?

Quick Answer

At sunset the sun is low, so light travels through much more air. Blue light scatters away before reaching you, leaving only red and orange to color the sky.

Let's Go Deeper

The same scattering that makes the sky blue also makes sunsets red. More atmosphere means more blue is filtered out. Dust and pollution can make sunsets even more vivid by adding extra scattering particles.

Try It Yourself

Add a drop of milk to a glass of water. Shine a torch through it. The far end glows orange — like sunset light traveling through thick air.

Ask This Next

Why is space black with billions of stars? → #12

#3 Why Does the Moon Change Shape?

Quick Answer

The moon doesn't change shape — we see different amounts of its sunlit side as it orbits Earth each month. It's our viewing angle changing, not the moon shrinking.

Let's Go Deeper

The moon takes 29.5 days to orbit Earth. As it moves, our viewing angle of its sunlit half changes. A full moon means Earth is between the sun and moon. A new moon means the moon is between Earth and the sun.

Try It Yourself

In a dark room, hold a ball and shine a torch at it from one side. Walk around it watching the lit portion change shape. That's the moon's phases.

Ask This Next

Why do we always see the same side of the moon? → #9

#4 Why Do We Have Day and Night?

Quick Answer

Earth spins like a top every 24 hours. The side facing the sun gets daylight. The side facing away gets night. You're spinning at 1,600 km/h right now.

Let's Go Deeper

Earth rotates west to east, which is why the sun appears to rise in the east and set in the west. Different countries experience day and night at different times. When it's noon in Singapore it's midnight in London.

Try It Yourself

Mark an X on a ball with a sticker. Shine a torch from one side and spin the ball. Watch your X move from light into darkness. That's one full day on Earth.

Ask This Next

Why do we have seasons? → #5

#5 Why Do We Have Seasons?

Quick Answer

Seasons happen because Earth is tilted at 23.5 degrees. In summer your half tilts toward the sun, getting more direct heat. In winter it tilts away.

Let's Go Deeper

It's NOT about distance from the sun — Earth is closest to the sun in January, during the Northern Hemisphere's winter. Seasons are about the angle sunlight hits the ground. Tilted sunlight spreads over more area and warms less.

Try It Yourself

Shine a torch straight down on paper — tight bright circle. Now tilt it — same light spreads into an oval. Tilted light is weaker. That's winter in action.

Ask This Next

Why do we have day and night? → #4

#6 Why Do Stars Twinkle?

Quick Answer

Stars don't actually twinkle. Their light wobbles as it passes through moving pockets of warm and cold air in our atmosphere before reaching your eyes.

Let's Go Deeper

Planets don't twinkle as much as stars because they're closer, appearing as tiny discs. Their wider light beam averages out the atmospheric wobble. Stars are so far away they appear as single points, making wobble very visible.

Try It Yourself

Look at a candle through a glass of water and gently stir. The flame shimmers — just like starlight shimmering through moving air layers above us.

Ask This Next

Why is space black with billions of stars? → #12

#7 Why Do Comets Have Tails?

Quick Answer

As a comet nears the sun, heat vaporizes its ice, releasing dust and gas. Solar wind blows this material into two glowing tails pointing away from the sun.

Let's Go Deeper

Comets have two tails. The dust tail curves gently behind the orbit path. The ion tail points directly away from the sun, pushed by solar wind. Even when a comet moves away, both tails still point away from the sun.

Try It Yourself

Hold a tissue in front of a hairdryer. No matter which way you move, the tissue always blows away from the dryer. Comet tails always point away from the sun.

Ask This Next

Why do shooting stars streak across the sky? → #11

#8 Why Do Planets Stay in Orbit?

Quick Answer

Planets fall toward the sun but move sideways so fast they keep missing it. Gravity pulls them in, momentum carries them forward — balanced into a perfect orbit.

Let's Go Deeper

Without gravity, planets would shoot off in straight lines forever. Without sideways momentum, they'd fall into the sun. Orbit is the perfect balance. The closer a planet is to the sun, the faster it must move to stay in orbit.

Try It Yourself

Tie a ball to a string and swing it in circles. The string is gravity. Let go and it flies straight — that's what happens without gravity keeping an orbit.

Ask This Next

Why do we have day and night? → #4

#9 Why Do We Always See the Same Side of the Moon?

Quick Answer

The moon spins at exactly the same speed it orbits Earth — so the same face always points our way. This is called tidal locking, and took millions of years.

Let's Go Deeper

Earth's gravity pulled on the moon's slight bulge over billions of years, slowing its spin until it matched its orbital speed. The far side of the moon wasn't photographed until 1959 when a Soviet spacecraft flew around it.

Try It Yourself

Walk in a circle around a chair while always facing it. You completed one rotation and one orbit — and the chair only ever saw your face. That's tidal locking.

? Ask This Next

Why does the moon change shape? → #3

#10 Why Is the Sun So Much Bigger Than It Looks?

Quick Answer

The sun looks small because it's 150 million km away. It's actually so big that 1.3 million Earths could fit inside it. Distance tricks your eyes completely.

Let's Go Deeper

Hold a coin at arm's length and it can cover the moon — yet the moon is 3,474 km wide. The sun is 400 times wider than the moon but 400 times further away, which is why they appear the same size during solar eclipses.

Try It Yourself

Hold a pea at arm's length. Look at a basketball 30m away. Both look similar in size. Distance creates illusions — the sun is that basketball.

Ask This Next

Why do planets stay in orbit? → #8

#11 Why Do Shooting Stars Streak Across the Sky?

Quick Answer

Shooting stars are small rocks burning up in our atmosphere. Friction with air heats them to thousands of degrees, making them glow as they vaporize completely.

Let's Go Deeper

Most shooting stars are no bigger than a grain of sand. They hit our atmosphere at up to 70 km per second and vaporize in seconds. On a clear night you can see 2-8 meteors per hour. During meteor showers, hundreds per hour are visible.

Try It Yourself

Rub your hands fast for 10 seconds — friction creates heat. Now imagine hitting air at 70 km per second. That creates thousands of degrees instantly.

Ask This Next

Why do comets have tails? → #7

#12 Why Is Space Black With Billions of Stars?

Quick Answer

Most stars are so far away their light is too faint to reach us. The universe is also only 13.8 billion years old — distant starlight simply hasn't arrived yet.

Let's Go Deeper

This puzzle is called Olbers' Paradox. If the universe were infinite and eternal, every line of sight would end at a star and the sky would glow white. But the universe has an age — so most starlight hasn't reached us yet.

Try It Yourself

Poke tiny holes in black card. Shine a torch behind it in a dark room. Bright spots on darkness — like stars. Darkness still dominates. That's our sky.

Ask This Next

Why would your blood boil in space? → #13

#13 Why Would Your Blood Boil in Space?

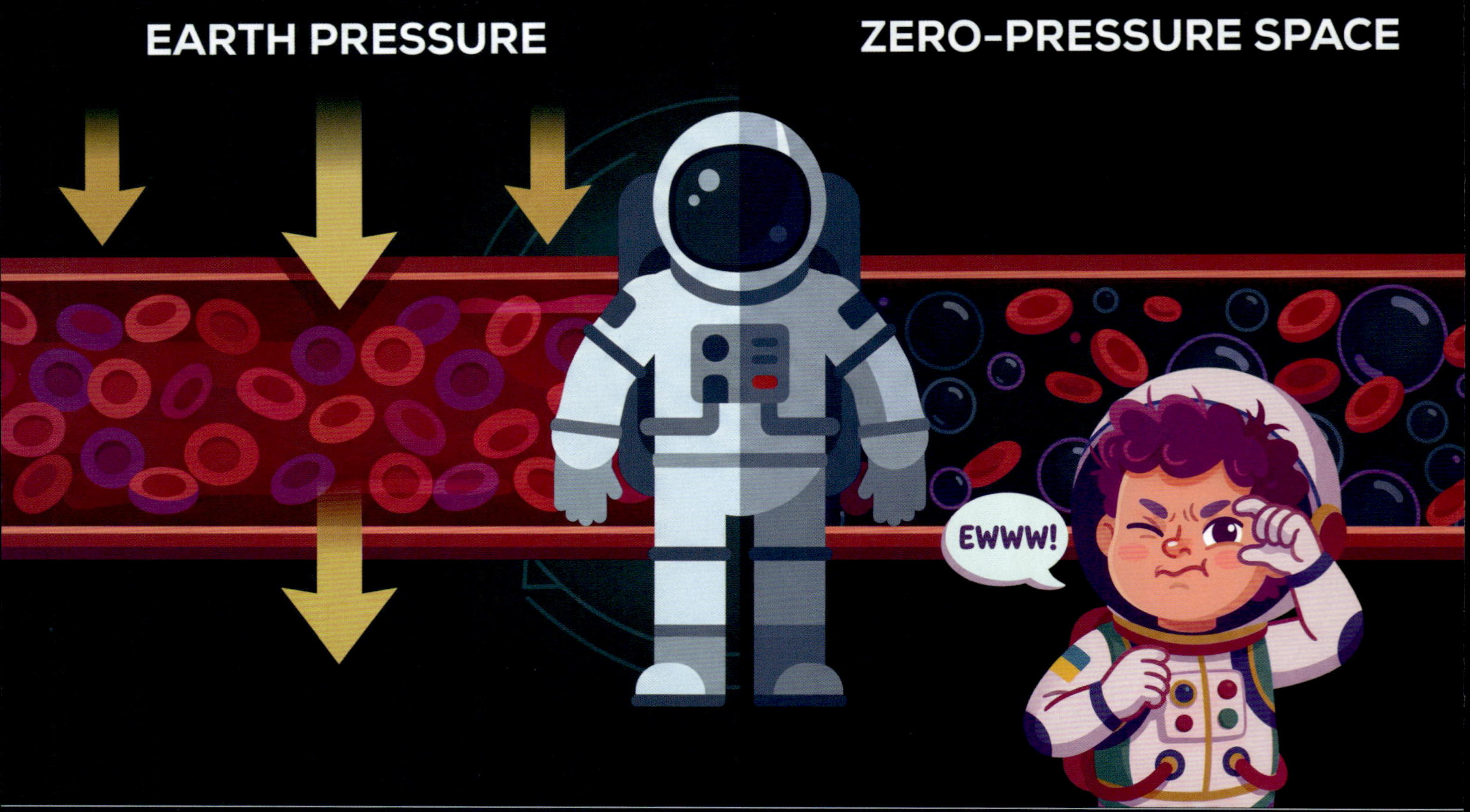

Quick Answer

In space there's almost no air pressure. Without pressure, liquids boil at body temperature. Your blood would form dangerous gas bubbles inside you without a spacesuit.

Let's Go Deeper

Boiling isn't just about heat — it's about pressure. At high altitude, water boils at lower temperatures because there's less air pressure. In the vacuum of space, pressure is near zero, so any liquid boils almost instantly.

Try It Yourself

Seal a syringe tip with your finger and pull the plunger back. Small bubbles appear without heat — just reduced pressure. That's space boiling in miniature.

Ask This Next

Why do astronauts grow taller in space? → #14

#14 Why Do Astronauts Grow Taller in Space?

Quick Answer

Gravity squishes the fluid-filled discs between your spine bones. In space, with no gravity, those discs expand and your spine stretches — up to 5cm taller.

Let's Go Deeper

You're slightly taller every morning than at night — gravity compresses your spine throughout the day. Astronauts returning from long missions must relearn walking as their spine readjusts. The growth reverses within days back on Earth.

Try It Yourself

Measure your height in the morning and before bed. Most people are 1-2 cm taller in the morning after spine decompression. Space makes this far more dramatic.

Ask This Next

Why would your blood boil in space? → #13

Chapter 2

Animals

Have you ever wondered why cats bring you dead mice as a gift, why sharks can never stop swimming, or why some animals eat their own poop? In this chapter we explore 16 of the most surprising questions about the animal kingdom — from the savanna to the deep ocean.

In this chapter:

#15 Why Do Sharks Never Stop Swimming?

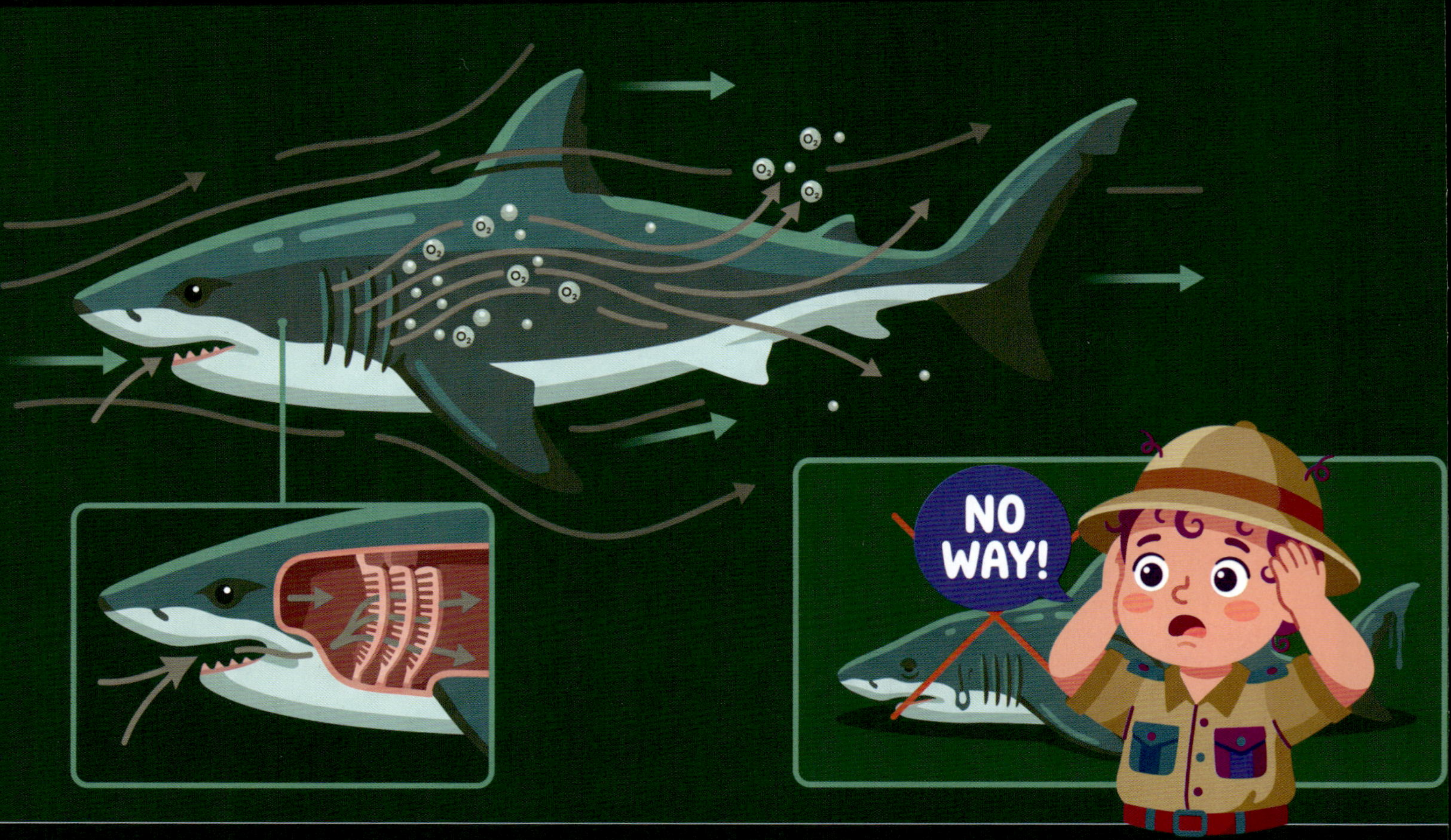

Quick Answer

Most sharks breathe by swimming — forward motion forces water over their gills extracting oxygen. If they stop moving, water stops flowing and they suffocate.

Let's Go Deeper

This is called ram ventilation. Some sharks like nurse sharks can pump water over their gills while stationary — but great whites and mako sharks cannot. They must keep moving 24 hours a day, even while sleeping. Sharks sleep by reducing brain activity while still swimming on autopilot.

Try It Yourself

Hold a paper fan still — no breeze. Move it back and forth — instant breeze. Ram ventilation sharks work the same way — motion creates the airflow to survive.

Ask This Next

Why do zebras have stripes? → #16

#16 Why Do Zebras Have Stripes?

⚡ Quick Answer

Zebra stripes confuse biting flies — the patterns make it hard for flies to land. Stripes may also help zebras recognise each other in a herd.

Let's Go Deeper

Scientists tested this by painting stripes on horses. Flies landed far less on striped horses than plain ones. The pattern disrupts the fly's landing approach. Stripes may also cool the zebra by creating tiny air currents across the skin.

Try It Yourself

Draw one plain paper animal and one striped. Ask someone to tap them quickly from a distance. The striped one is harder to aim at. Patterns confuse targeting.

❓ Ask This Next

Why do some animals eat their own poop?
→ #28

#17 Why Do Cats Purr?

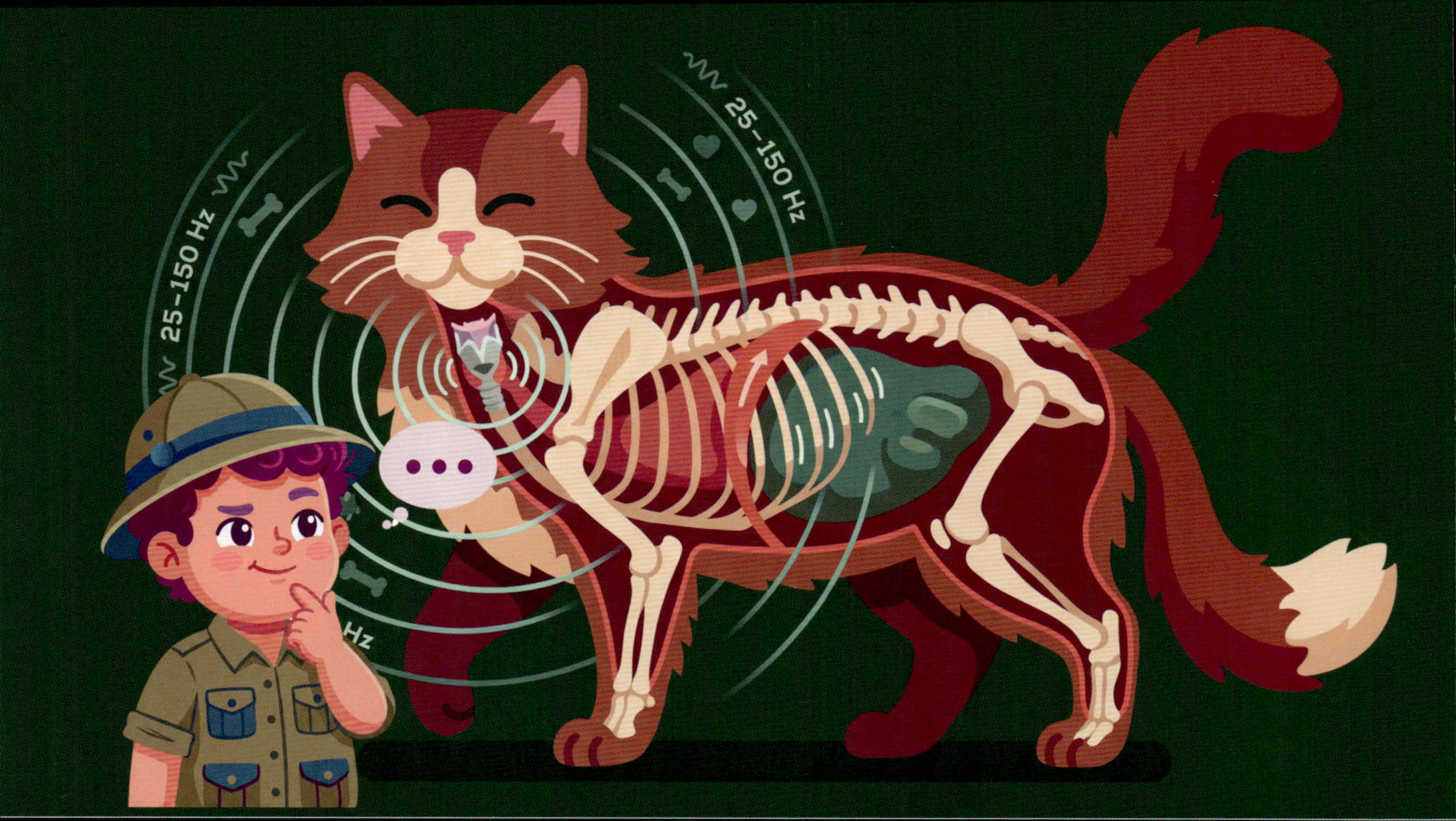

Quick Answer

Cats purr by rapidly contracting larynx muscles 25-150 times per second. It signals contentment but also generates healing frequencies that strengthen their own bones.

Let's Go Deeper

Purring frequencies between 25-50 Hz have been shown to promote bone density and healing. Cats often purr when injured or stressed — not just happy. It may be a self-soothing mechanism that evolved to keep bones strong during rest.

Try It Yourself

Put your hand on a purring cat's throat and feel the vibrations. Now hum low — you're making a similar vibration in your own throat the same way.

Ask This Next

Why do dogs tilt their heads? → #26

#18 Why Do Birds Sing?

⚡ Quick Answer

Birds sing mainly to claim territory and attract mates. Each species has a unique song. Males mostly sing at dawn when sound travels furthest in cool still air.

Let's Go Deeper

Bird songs are learned, not instinct — young birds listen to adults and practice. Some birds like the lyrebird can mimic chainsaws and cameras. The dawn chorus happens because cool morning air carries sound further, making singing more effective.

Try It Yourself

Go outside at dawn and count distinct bird songs you can hear. Each different pattern is a species claiming territory. Try recording them to compare later.

? Ask This Next

Why do fireflies glow? → #23

#19 Why Do Bees Make Honey?

Quick Answer

Bees make honey as a winter food store. They collect nectar from flowers, add enzymes, evaporate the water by fanning it, then seal it in wax cells. It lasts forever.

Let's Go Deeper

A single bee produces only 1/12 teaspoon of honey in its lifetime. A hive needs around 40kg of honey to survive winter. Honey's low moisture and high acidity prevent bacteria — archaeologists have found edible honey in ancient Egyptian tombs.

Try It Yourself

Put sugar water in a shallow dish in the sun for an hour. Check how much water evaporates. Bees do this inside the hive by fanning with their wings.

Ask This Next

Why do fireflies glow? → #23

#20 Why Do Animals Hibernate?

Quick Answer

When food disappears in winter, hibernating animals slow everything down — heartbeat, breathing, body temperature — to survive on stored fat for months without eating.

Let's Go Deeper

A hibernating hedgehog's heart rate drops from 190 to just 5 beats per minute. Body temperature can fall close to freezing. True hibernators are almost impossible to wake. Bears actually sleep lightly — they can wake if disturbed — so they are not true hibernators.

Try It Yourself

Count your breaths per minute normally. Hibernating animals drop from 20 breaths to just 1. Hold your breath to feel how dramatic that slowdown really is.

Ask This Next

Why do cats purr? → #17

#21 Why Do Spiders Spin Webs?

Quick Answer

Spiders spin webs to catch food using silk from their abdomen — stronger than steel by weight. They also use silk for shelter, egg sacs and ballooning on wind.

Let's Go Deeper

Spider silk is one of the strongest materials on Earth — five times stronger than steel by weight and stretchier than nylon. The spiral sticky threads catch prey while the radial frame threads the spider walks on are not sticky. Spiders know which threads to avoid.

Try It Yourself

Find a dewy spiderweb and touch the spiral and radial threads. Spirals are sticky, radials are not. The spider navigates its own trap using that difference.

Ask This Next

Why do fireflies glow? → #23

#22 Why Do Snakes Shed Skin?

Quick Answer

Snakes shed their entire skin in one piece because their scales don't grow with them. As they get bigger, they grow a new layer underneath then wriggle out of the old one.

Let's Go Deeper

Before shedding, a snake's eyes turn blue and cloudy as fluid builds between the old and new skin. Young snakes shed every few weeks because they grow fast. Old snakes shed a few times a year. The shed skin is a perfect transparent copy of the whole snake.

Try It Yourself

Pull a tight glove inside-out over your hand. It peels from the fingertip backward in one piece — exactly how a snake exits its old skin from nose to tail.

Ask This Next

Why can a jellyfish sting you when it's dead? → #30

#23 Why Do Fireflies Glow?

Quick Answer

Fireflies glow to find mates using a chemical reaction that produces almost no heat — the most efficient light on Earth. Each species has its own unique flash code.

Let's Go Deeper

Firefly light is called bioluminescence — a chemical reaction between luciferin and oxygen. Unlike light bulbs which waste 90% of energy as heat, firefly light is almost 100% efficient. Some female fireflies mimic other species' flash codes to lure and eat males.

Try It Yourself

Crack a glow stick in a dark room and feel how cool it stays. Like fireflies, it makes light through chemistry with almost no heat wasted.

Ask This Next

Why do cats bring you dead animals? → #29

#24 Why Do Elephants Have Big Ears?

Quick Answer

Elephant ears are full of blood vessels. Flapping them cools blood before it returns to the body. African elephants have bigger ears because their habitat is hotter.

Let's Go Deeper

An elephant can lower its body temperature by up to 10 degrees just by flapping its ears. Asian elephants live in cooler forests and have much smaller ears. The ear shape also roughly maps the continent — African elephant ears are shaped like Africa.

Try It Yourself

Wet your hand and fan it — it cools fast from evaporation. Elephant ears cool blood vessels near the skin surface in exactly the same way.

Ask This Next

Why do some fish swim in schools? → #27

#25 Why Do Fish Need Water to Breathe?

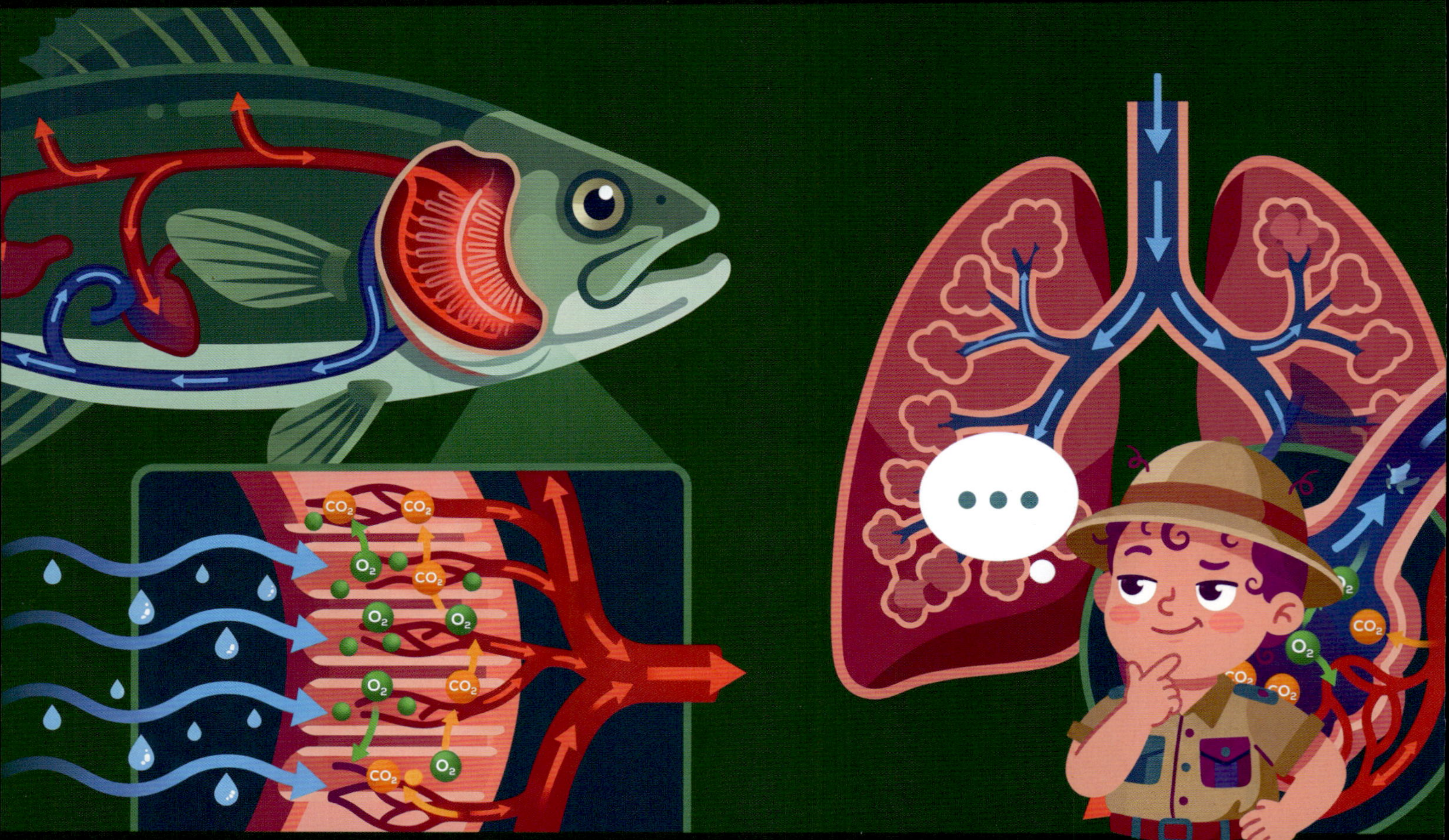

Quick Answer

Fish breathe dissolved oxygen in water using gills. Water flows over gill filaments and oxygen passes into the bloodstream — the same process as lungs but underwater.

Let's Go Deeper

Water contains dissolved oxygen — about 1/30th as much as air. Fish gills are extremely efficient at extracting it. Warm water holds less oxygen, which is why fish gasp at the surface in hot weather. Some fish like lungfish can breathe both air and water.

Try It Yourself

Stir sugar into water until it vanishes. Dissolved but invisible. Fish breathe oxygen dissolved in water the same invisible way, extracting it through gills.

Ask This Next

Why do some animals eat their own poop? → #28

#26 Why Do Dogs Tilt Their Heads?

Quick Answer

Dogs tilt their heads to better locate sounds and see past their snout to read your face. It repositions their ears for more accurate sound triangulation.

Let's Go Deeper

Dogs with longer snouts tilt more than flat-faced breeds because the snout blocks their view of a speaker's mouth. Research shows dogs tilt most when they hear meaningful words they know. It also may signal focused attention — showing you they're listening carefully.

Try It Yourself

Cup your hands behind your ears and listen — sound improves. Tilt your head slowly while listening. The direction shifts. Dogs use that tilt to locate sounds.

Ask This Next

Why do cats bring you dead animals? → #29

#27 Why Do Some Fish Swim in Schools?

Quick Answer

Schools confuse predators — thousands of identical moving fish are impossible to target. Each fish also gets instant danger warnings from neighbors, moving the whole group as one.

Let's Go Deeper

Each fish watches its immediate neighbors and copies their movement with a tiny delay — creating rippling waves through the school that confuse predators. A predator trying to pick one fish from thousands of identical moving targets suffers a confusion effect called the dazzle effect.

Try It Yourself

Look at a page of identical dots and quickly point to just one. Hard when everything matches — that's the confusion a predator faces attacking a fish school.

Ask This Next

Why do some animals eat their own poop?
→ #28

#28 Why Do Some Animals Eat Their Own Poop?

Quick Answer

Rabbits eat soft pellets straight from their body — not regular droppings. These pellets contain nutrients their gut missed the first time. It's efficient recycling, not gross.

Let's Go Deeper

Rabbits produce two types of droppings — hard dry pellets they leave behind, and soft cecotropes eaten straight from the body, often at night. Cecotropes contain bacteria, vitamins and proteins from fermentation. Without eating them, rabbits would become malnourished.

Try It Yourself

Compost a banana peel in soil for two weeks. Bacteria unlock nutrients locked inside. Rabbit cecotropes do the same job inside the body on a second pass.

Ask This Next

Why do cats bring you dead animals? → #29

#29 Why Do Cats Bring You Dead Animals?

Quick Answer

Cats think of you as a large helpless kitten who can't hunt. Bringing prey is a gift — the same instinct mother cats use to feed and teach their real kittens.

Let's Go Deeper

Mother cats bring live prey to kittens to teach hunting skills. Domestic cats extend this behavior to their human family. Well-fed cats hunt more than hungry ones — it's instinct not appetite. Cats that bring live prey may actually be trying to teach you.

Try It Yourself

When a cat brings you something, react warmly instead of shrieking. From the cat's view it just did something kind. Your disgust genuinely confuses it.

Ask This Next

Why can a jellyfish sting you when it's dead? → #30

#30 Why Can a Jellyfish Sting You When It's Dead?

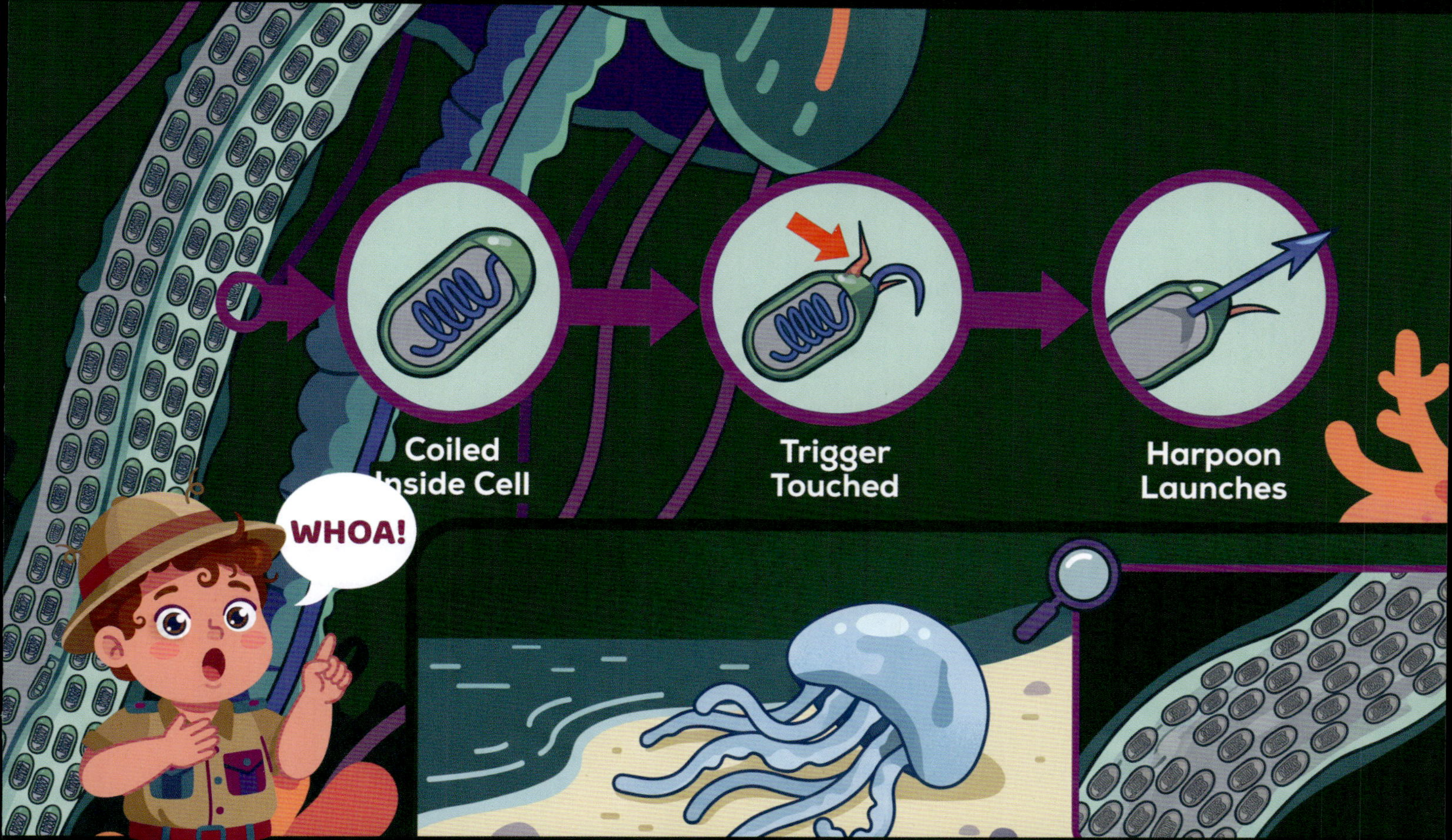

⚡ Quick Answer

Jellyfish sting with spring-loaded harpoon cells called nematocysts that fire when touched. These stay loaded and active even after the jellyfish dies.

Let's Go Deeper

Nematocysts are among the fastest biological mechanisms on Earth — firing in under 700 nanoseconds. The harpoon launches, pierces skin and injects venom before you can feel it. Dead jellyfish washed ashore can still sting for hours. Even separated tentacle fragments remain dangerous.

Try It Yourself

Set a mousetrap and walk away. It stays loaded and fires when touched — no mouse needed. Dead jellyfish nematocysts work exactly the same way.

? Ask This Next

Why do snakes shed their skin? → #21

Chapter 3

Human Body

Have you ever wondered why papercuts hurt more than big scrapes, why your eyes move when you dream, or what poop is actually made of? In this chapter we explore 14 of the most surprising — and occasionally disgusting — questions about the body you live in.

In this chapter:

#31 Why Do We Yawn — And Why Is It Contagious?

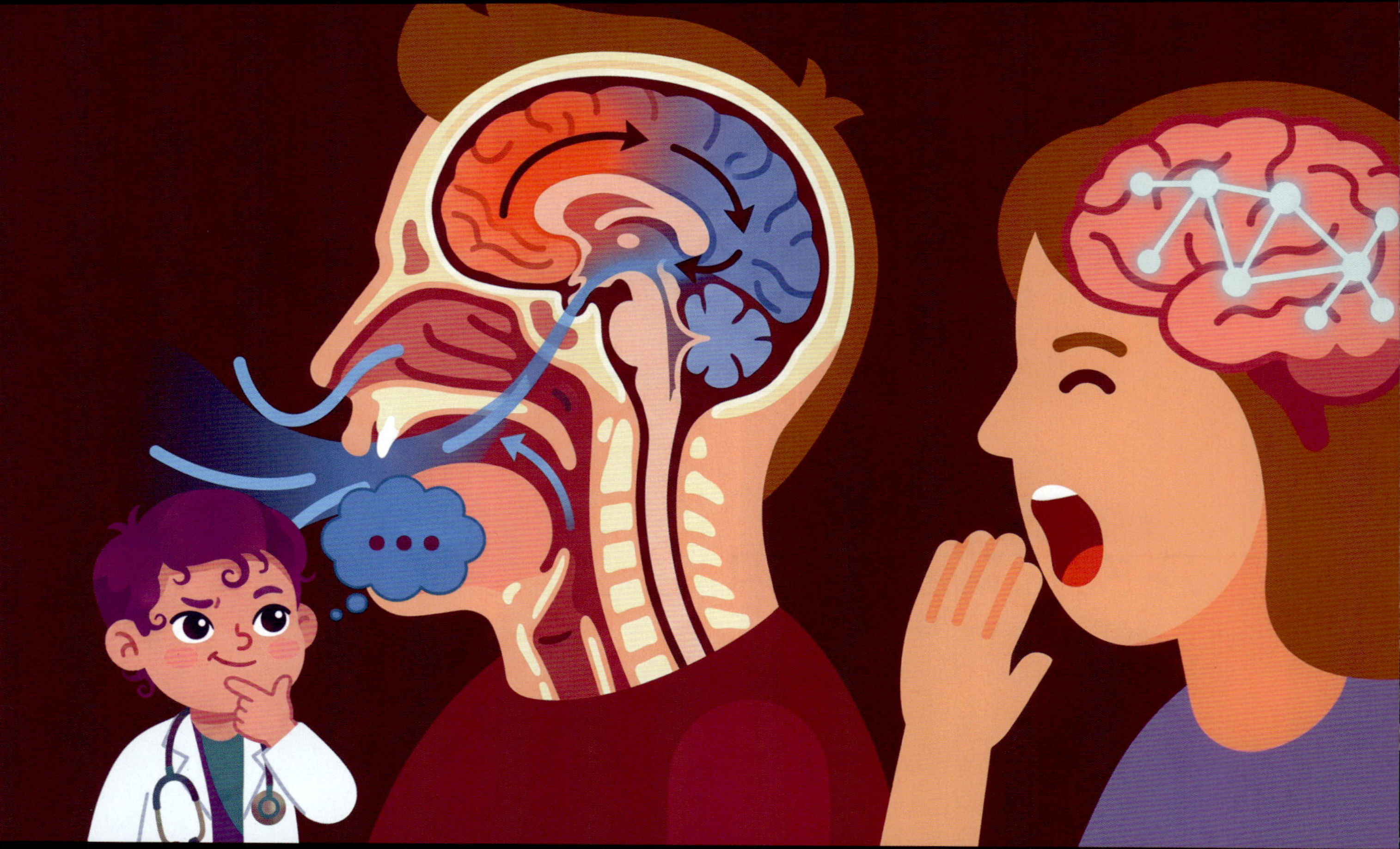

Quick Answer
Yawning may cool your brain by bringing in fresh air. It's contagious because seeing someone yawn triggers mirror neurons — the same cells that make you feel what others feel.

Let's Go Deeper
Scientists found that people yawn more when their brain temperature rises. Yawning brings cooler outside air into contact with blood vessels near the mouth. Contagious yawning is linked to empathy — people with higher empathy catch yawns more easily. Even reading the word yawn can trigger one.

Try It Yourself
Read this slowly: yawn... yawn... yawn. Did it work? Try it on a family member. Contagious yawning works through text — your brain mirrors others.

? Ask This Next
Why do we dream? → #32

#32 Why Do We Dream?

Quick Answer

Dreams happen mainly during REM sleep when your brain is almost as active as when awake. Scientists think dreaming helps sort and store memories and process emotions from the day.

Let's Go Deeper

During REM sleep, your brain replays and reorganises experiences, strengthening important memories and discarding others. The prefrontal cortex — your logical brain — is less active, which is why dreams feel strange and real at the same time. Dreams may also help us rehearse responses to threats.

Try It Yourself

Keep a notebook by your bed. Write dream memories the moment you wake. After a week notice which people appear most — that's what your brain processes.

Ask This Next

Why do your eyes move while you dream?
→ #41

#33 Why Does Our Heart Beat?

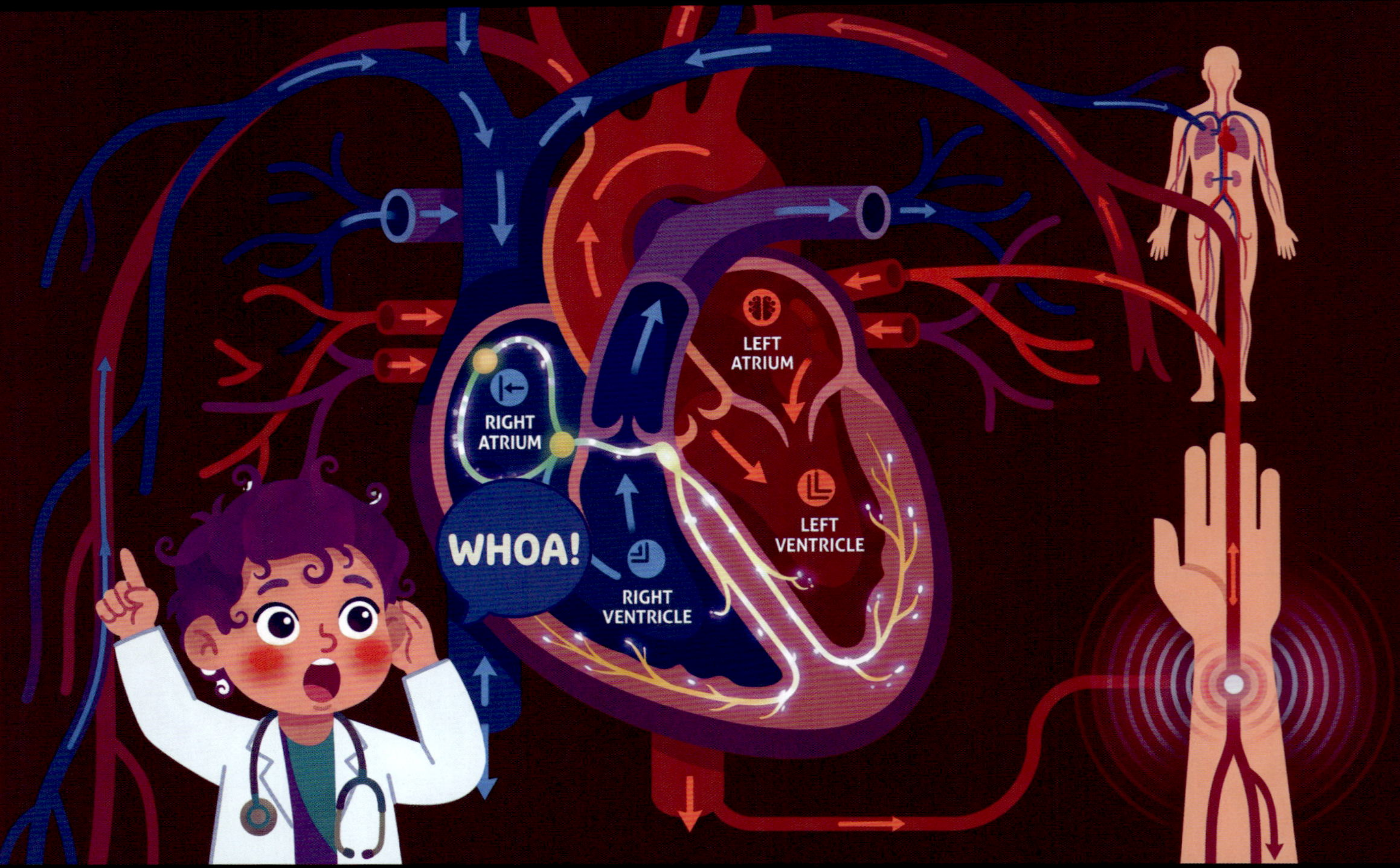

⚡ Quick Answer

Your heart beats from its own built-in pacemaker — the sinoatrial node. This tiny cluster fires about 100,000 times a day with no instruction needed from your brain.

Let's Go Deeper

The heart has its own electrical system independent of the brain. The sinoatrial node sends a signal that travels through the heart muscle, making chambers contract in sequence — atria first, then ventricles. This is why a heart can keep beating briefly outside the body.

Try It Yourself

Press two fingers on your wrist. Count pulses for 15 seconds and multiply by four. Do 20 jumping jacks and count again. Your heart adjusted automatically.

? Ask This Next

Why do we need sleep? → #34

#34 Why Do We Need Sleep?

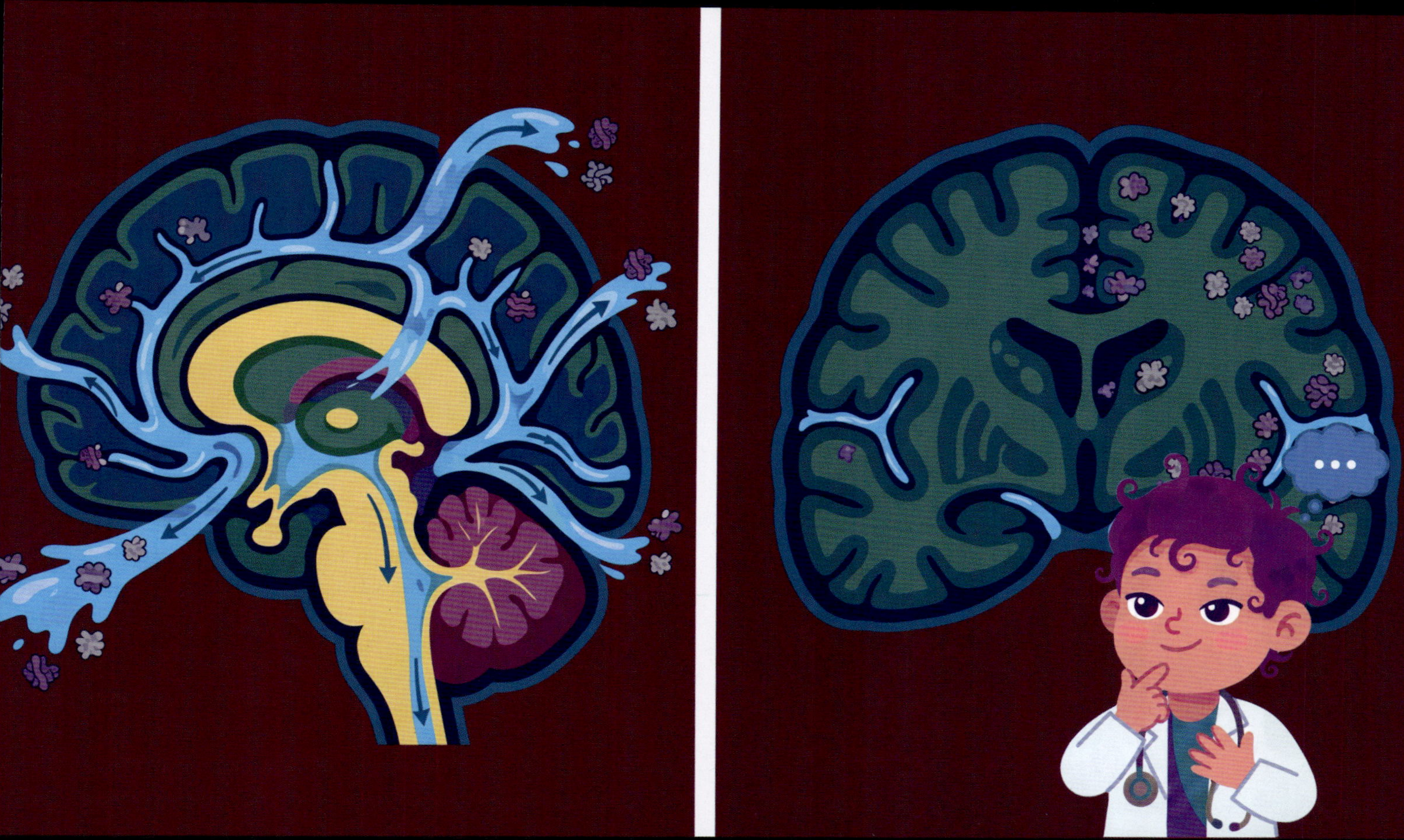

Quick Answer

Sleep is when your brain washes itself — flushing toxic waste proteins that build up all day. Without sleep this waste accumulates and causes lasting damage to brain tissue.

Let's Go Deeper

During sleep, brain cells shrink by 60%, creating channels for cerebrospinal fluid to flush out waste including beta-amyloid — a protein linked to Alzheimer's disease. Memory consolidation, immune repair and growth hormone release also happen mainly during sleep.

Try It Yourself

Test your reaction time on a phone app before bed then after sleeping well. Sleep-deprived reactions resemble being drunk. Sleep makes your brain cleaner.

Ask This Next

Why do we dream? → #32

#35 Why Do We Have a Belly Button?

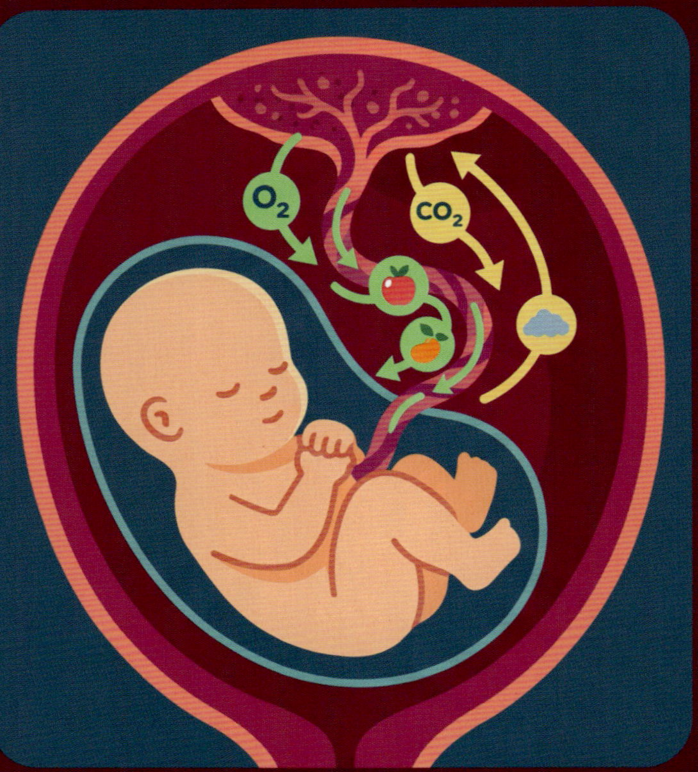

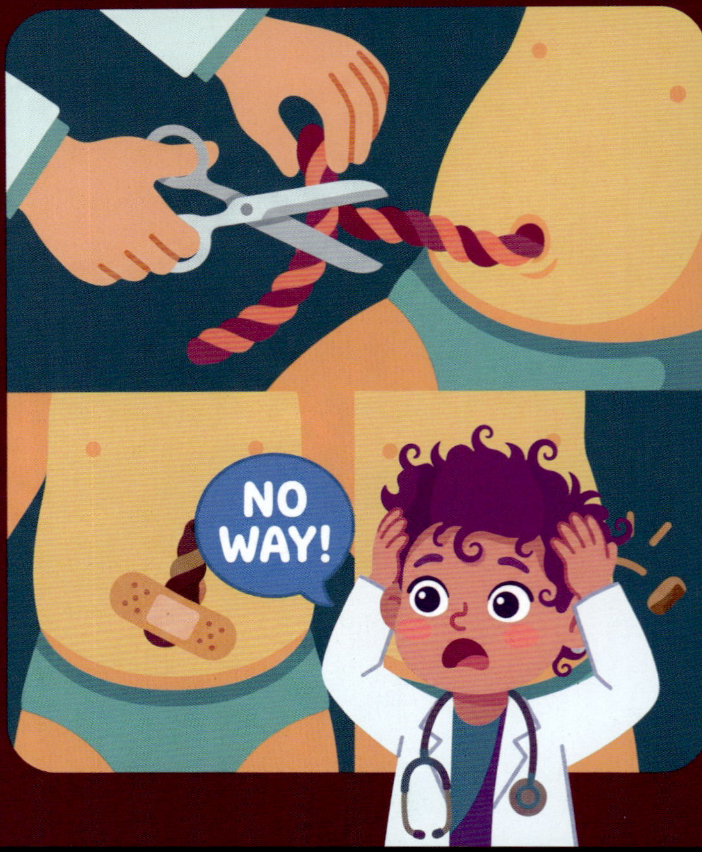

Quick Answer

Your belly button is the scar where your umbilical cord was attached before birth. The cord connected you to your mother and delivered all your food and oxygen for nine months.

Let's Go Deeper

Before birth you couldn't breathe or eat — the umbilical cord carried oxygen and nutrients from the placenta directly into your bloodstream. After birth the cord is clamped and cut. The stump dries and falls off within weeks, leaving the belly button scar. Innies and outies depend on how the stump healed.

Try It Yourself

Look at your belly button — the oldest scar on your body. Compare innies and outies with family. Shape depends on how skin healed, not how the cord was cut.

Ask This Next

Why do fingers wrinkle in water? → #37

#36 Why Do We Get Goosebumps?

Quick Answer

Goosebumps happen when tiny muscles pull your hair upright. In furry ancestors this trapped warmth and made them look bigger. We kept the reflex but lost most of the fur.

Let's Go Deeper

Tiny muscles called arrector pili attach to each hair follicle. Triggered by cold or strong emotion, they contract and pull the hair upright. In animals with thick fur this creates an insulating air layer or a threat display. In humans with little hair it just makes small bumps on the skin.

Try It Yourself

Hold ice on your arm for 10 seconds and watch goosebumps appear. Now listen to music that gives you chills. Same reflex — triggered by cold and by emotion.

Ask This Next

Why do we get hiccups? → #39

#37 Why Do Fingers Wrinkle in Water?

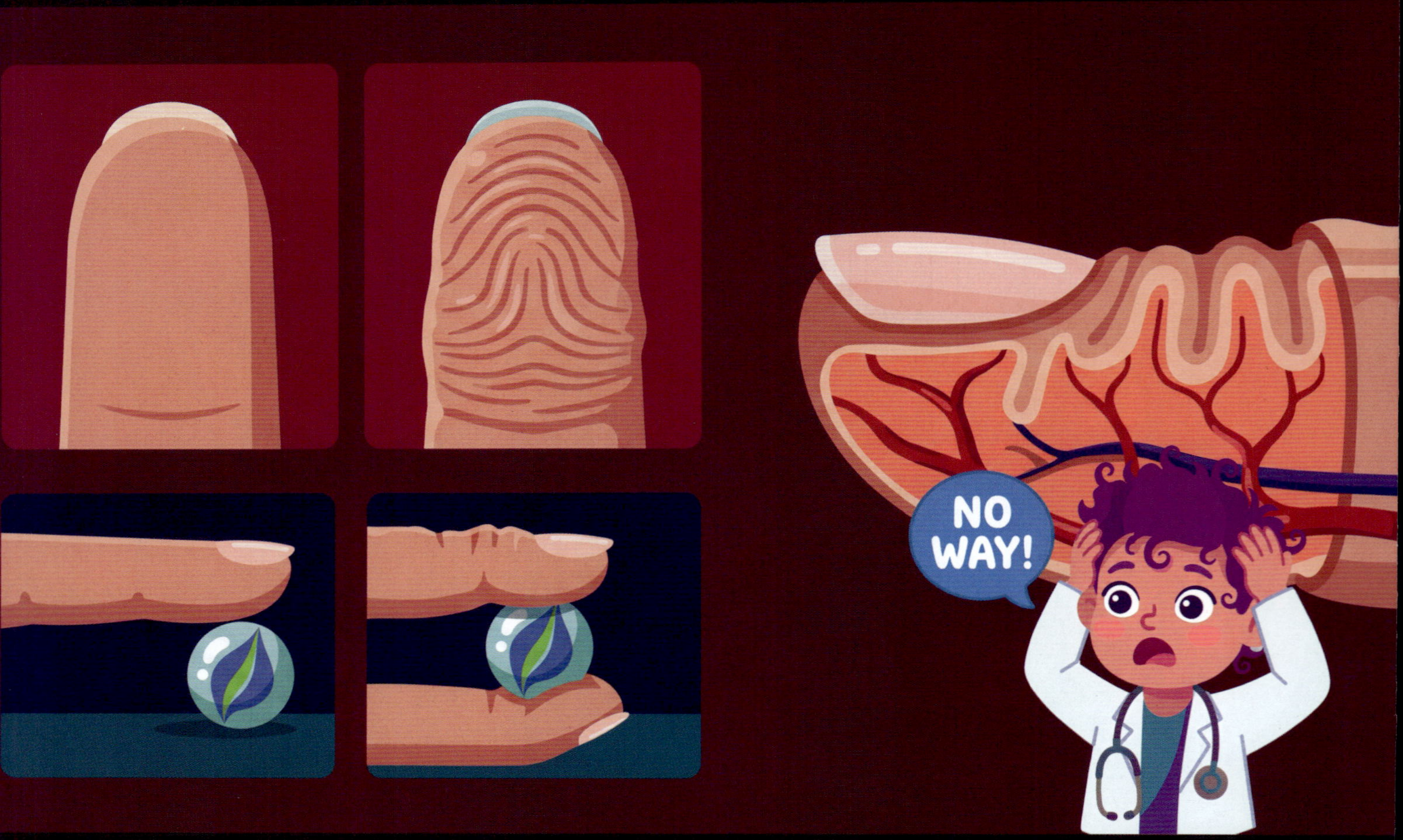

Quick Answer

Finger wrinkling is not waterlogging — your nervous system deliberately contracts blood vessels to create grip channels. It's an evolutionary tool for handling wet objects.

Let's Go Deeper

Scientists proved this is active not passive — people with nerve damage don't wrinkle even after hours soaking. The nervous system detects water and triggers blood vessel contraction, creating ridges that improve grip on wet surfaces like rocks or rain-soaked food.

Try It Yourself

Soak your hands 5 minutes then pick up wet soap. Compare with dry hands. Wrinkled fingers grip wet objects better — your body solved a problem automatically.

Ask This Next

Why does a papercut hurt more than a big scrape? → #40

#38 Why Do Bones Break But Heal Themselves?

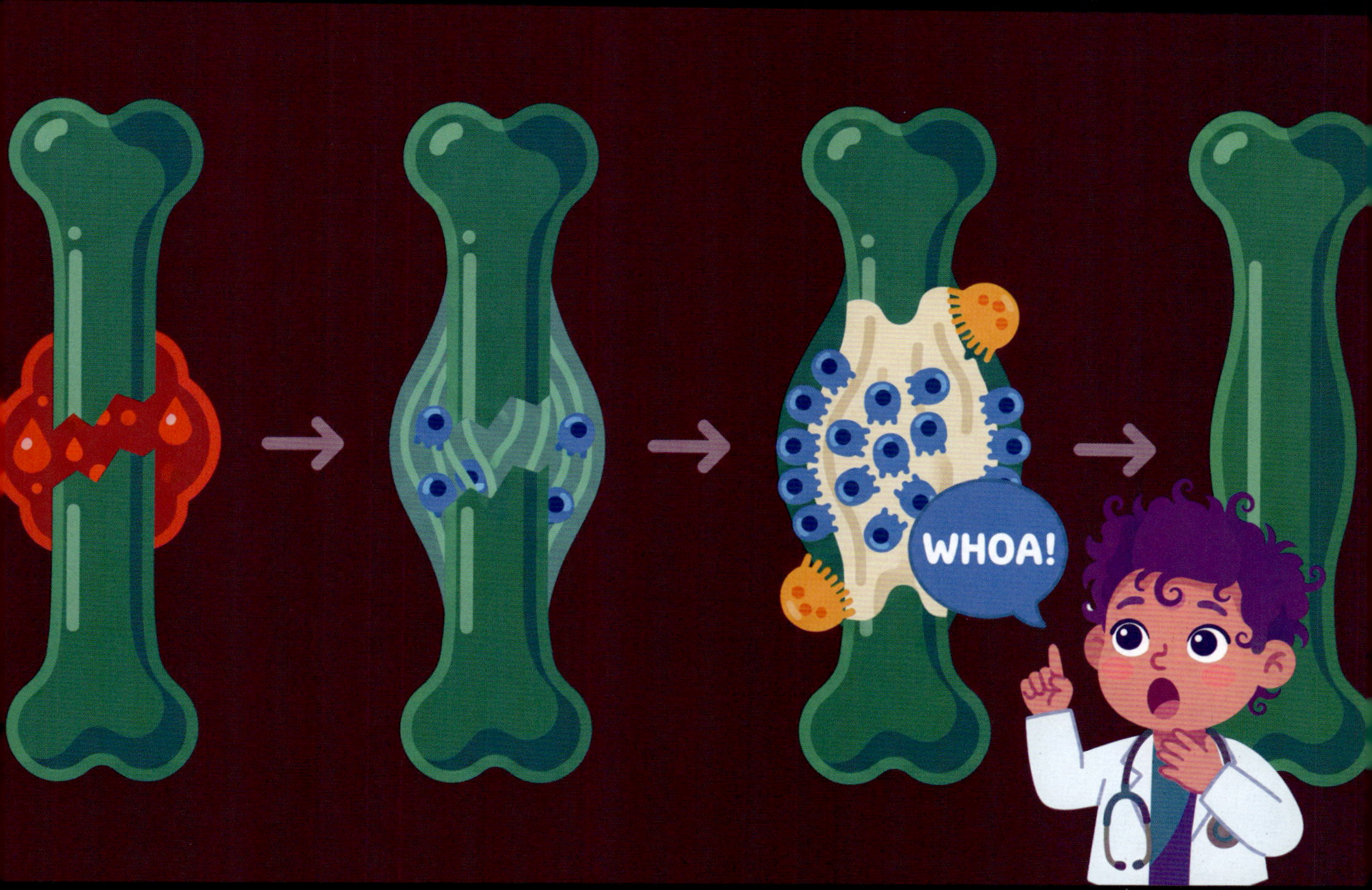

Quick Answer

Bones heal because they contain living cells. Osteoblasts build new bone while osteoclasts clear damage. A healed fracture is often stronger than the original bone was.

Let's Go Deeper

Within hours of a break, a blood clot forms as scaffolding. Osteoblasts migrate to the site and start depositing new bone material. Over weeks a bony callus bridges the gap. Over months osteoclasts reshape it until it's almost indistinguishable from original bone, often denser at the fracture site.

Try It Yourself

Soak a chicken bone in vinegar for three days — it goes rubbery as the calcium dissolves. Bone needs both minerals for hardness and collagen for flexibility.

Ask This Next

Why do we get hiccups? → #39

#39 Why Do We Get Hiccups?

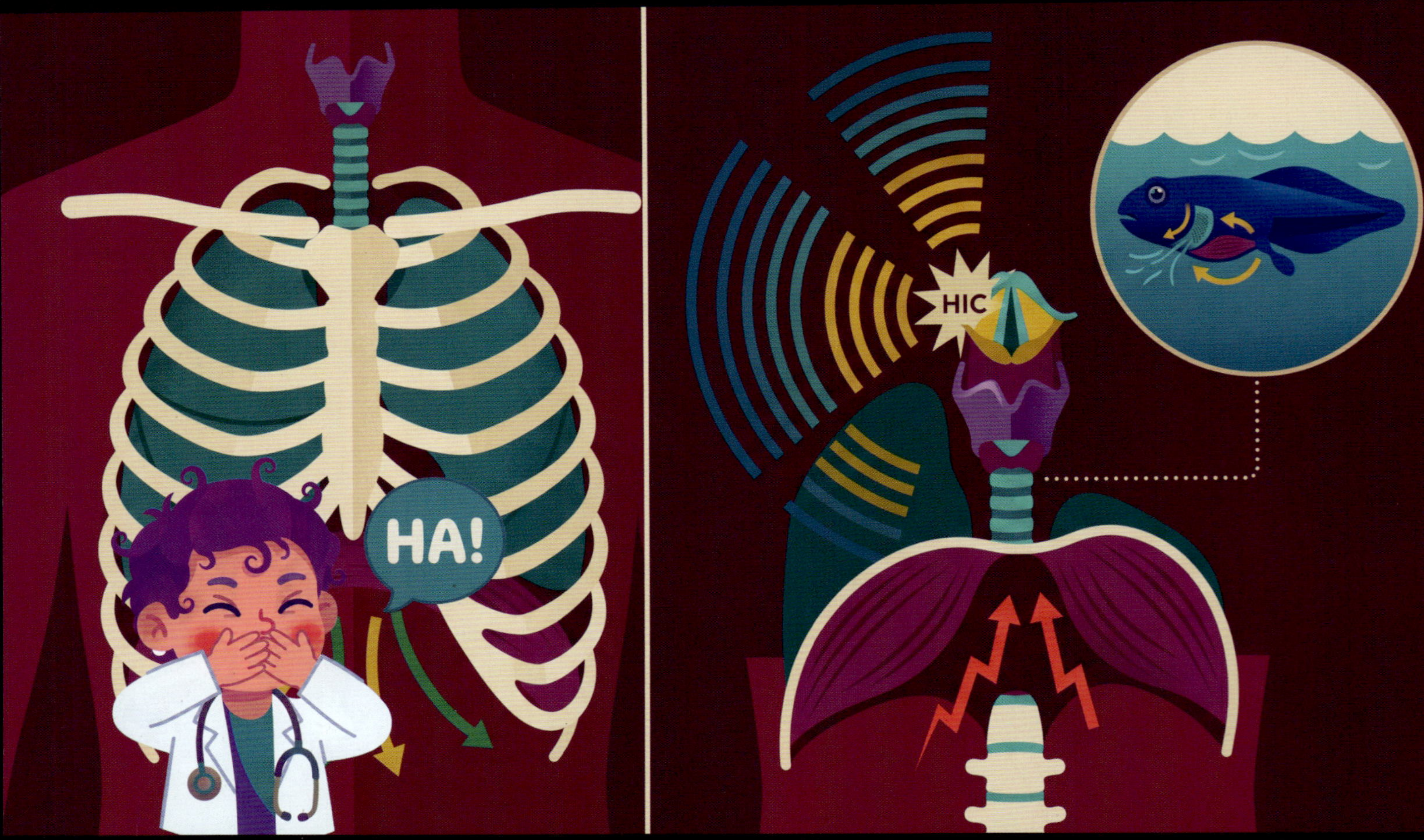

Quick Answer
Hiccups are diaphragm spasms causing a sharp inhale. The glottis snaps shut making the HIC sound. Scientists think it is an ancient reflex we inherited from fish ancestors.

Let's Go Deeper
The hiccup reflex may date back 375 million years when our amphibian ancestors used it to push water over their gills. In humans it serves no useful purpose. Eating too fast, swallowing air, or temperature changes can trigger it. Most cases resolve in minutes — the longest recorded lasted 68 years.

Try It Yourself
Try every hiccup cure — holding breath, drinking upside down, being startled. Most work by raising blood CO2 which overrides the diaphragm spasm reflex signal.

Ask This Next
Why do we yawn? → #31

#40 Why Does a Papercut Hurt More Than a Big Scrape?

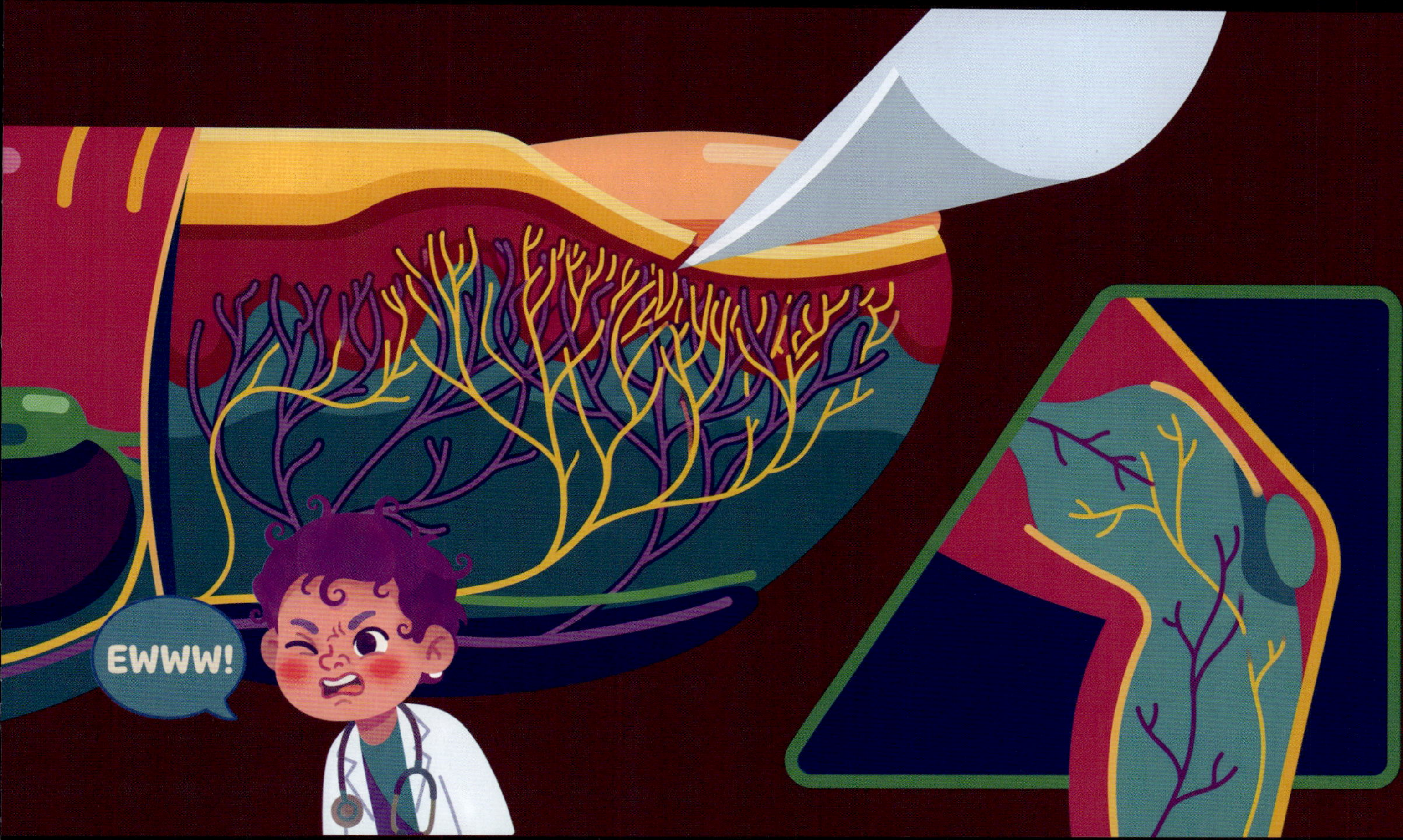

Quick Answer

Fingertips have more pain receptors than almost anywhere. A papercut hits maximum nerve depth without going deep enough to trigger the numbing endorphins that dull bigger wounds.

Let's Go Deeper

Fingertips need extreme sensitivity for fine motor tasks — we have over 2,500 touch receptors per square centimetre there. Papercuts are also shallow enough to stay open and exposed to air, which keeps pain receptors firing continuously. Large wounds trigger more endorphin release which dulls the pain faster.

Try It Yourself

Touch two toothpick tips on your fingertip — feel two points. Try your back — feel one. Fingertips detect 2mm. Backs need 70mm. That explains papercut pain.

Ask This Next

Why do your eyes move while you dream?
→ #41

#41 Why Do Your Eyes Move While You Dream?

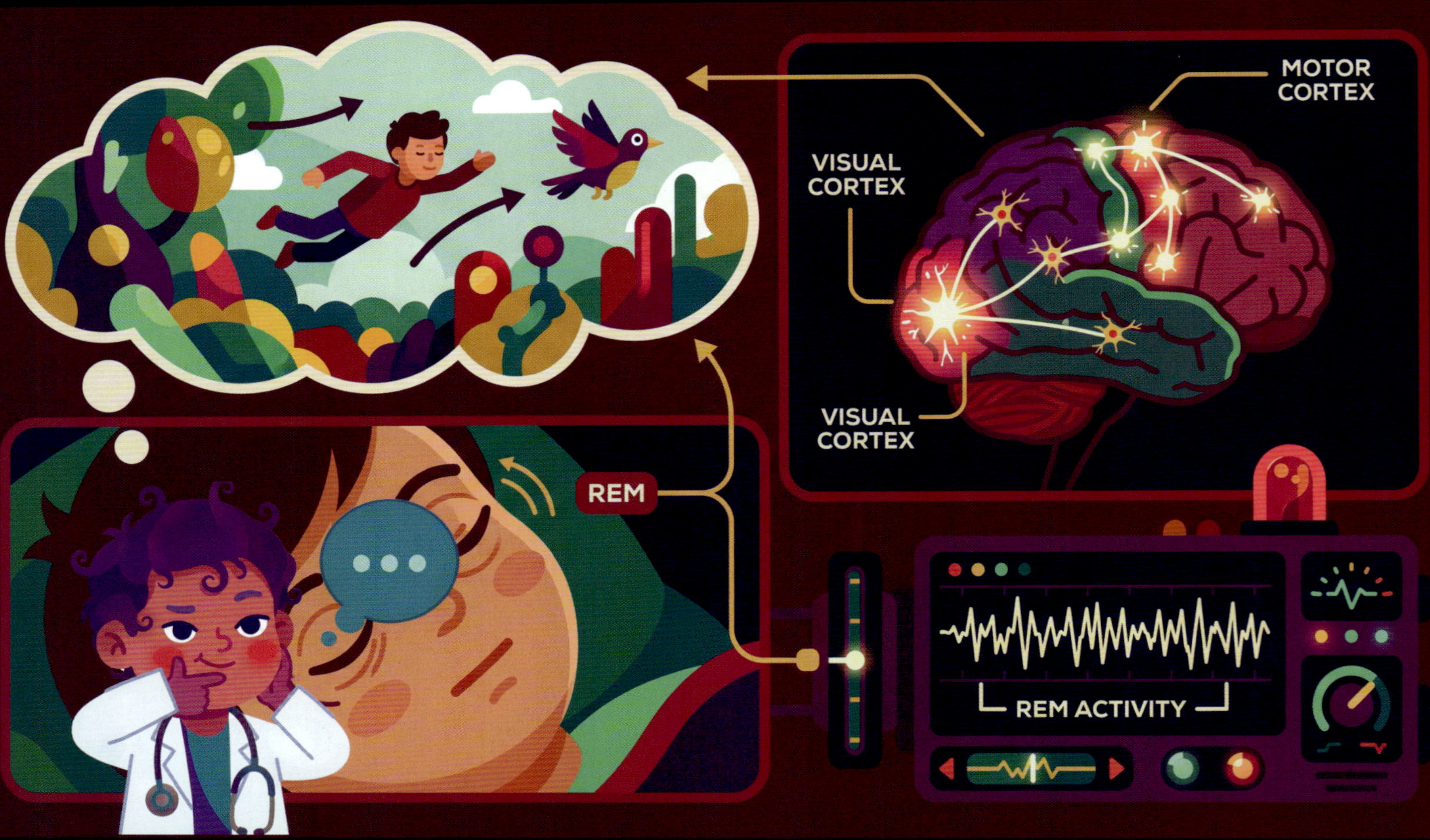

Quick Answer

During REM sleep your brain generates vivid dreams and your eyes track the action as if watching a real scene. Eye movements correspond to where you look inside the dream.

Let's Go Deeper

REM stands for Rapid Eye Movement. The visual cortex is nearly as active as when awake. Researchers map dream content by recording eye movements — repeated left-right movement suggests watching something move. Most muscles are paralysed during REM but eyes are the exception.

Try It Yourself

Watch someone sleep in low light for eyes moving under their eyelids. Gently wake them during movement — they will almost always report a vivid dream happening.

Ask This Next

Why does snot turn green when sick? → #42

#42 Why Does Snot Turn Green When You're Sick?

Quick Answer

Green snot is dead white blood cells. When sick your immune system floods your nose with defenders. As they die fighting infection they release a green enzyme — myeloperoxidase.

Let's Go Deeper

Mucus traps dust and bacteria daily, draining quietly down the throat. During infection white blood cells rush in. The green colour comes from myeloperoxidase, an iron-containing enzyme in dying neutrophils. Green snot means your immune system is winning.

Try It Yourself

Blow your nose day one of a cold — clear. Day three — green. You are watching your immune battle live. Green means white blood cells are winning the fight.

Ask This Next

Why do farts make a sound? → #43

#43 Why Do Farts Make a Sound?

Quick Answer

Gas builds up in intestines and squeezes out through a small opening, making the skin vibrate like a raspberry. Tighter opening means higher pitch. More gas means louder sound.

Let's Go Deeper

Gut bacteria break down food releasing nitrogen, carbon dioxide and small amounts of sulfur compounds. Sound happens as gas pushes through the sphincter — tighter means higher pitch. About 99% of fart gas is odorless. Only the tiny sulfur fraction smells.

Try It Yourself

Blow a balloon and stretch its neck. Tight stretch squeaks high. Loose stretch sounds lower. That is exactly your body's own mechanism every single time.

Ask This Next

Why Do Some Farts Smell So Much Worse? → #85

#44 Why Does Poop Smell – And What Is It Made Of?

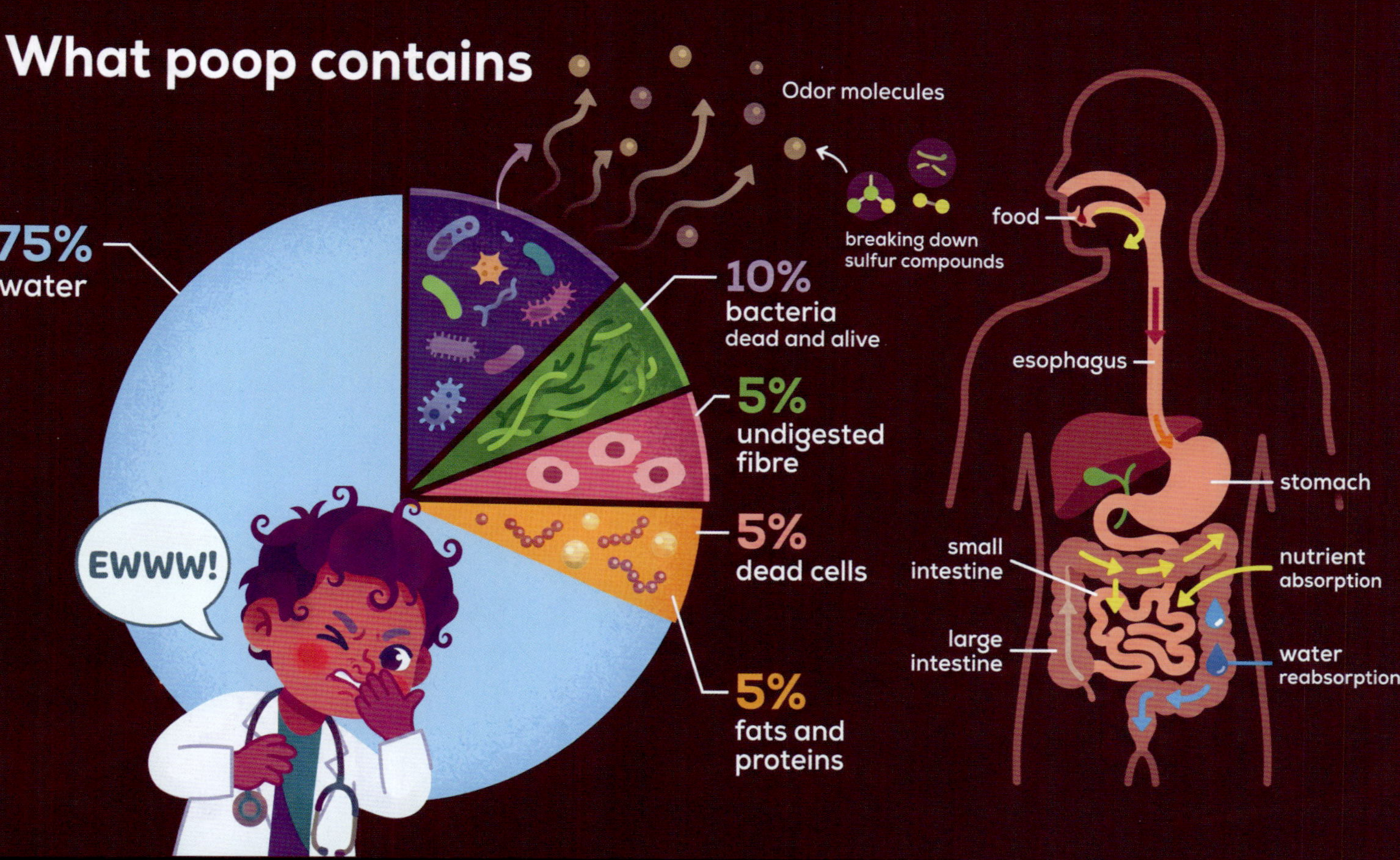

Quick Answer

Poop is 75% water. The rest is dead gut bacteria, undigested fibre, dead cells and fat. The smell comes from sulfur compounds bacteria produce breaking down food.

Let's Go Deeper

Gut bacteria ferment undigested food producing hydrogen sulfide — the smell of rotten eggs. High protein diets produce more sulfur compounds. About a third of dry poop weight is microbial life — living and dead bacteria from your gut.

Try It Yourself

Notice the smell after vegetables versus meat. You smell sulfur compounds bacteria produce breaking down protein. Your diet determines the smell completely.

Ask This Next

Why does food go bad? → #82

Chapter 4

Nature & Earth

Have you ever wondered why volcanoes erupt, how quicksand can swallow you whole, or why some plants actually eat insects? In this chapter we explore 16 of the most dramatic questions about the planet we live on — from the molten core beneath your feet to the storm clouds above your head.

In this chapter:

#45 Why Does It Rain?

Quick Answer

Water evaporates from oceans and lakes, rises as vapor, cools into clouds, then falls as rain when droplets grow too heavy. The same water has been cycling for billions of years.

Let's Go Deeper

The sun heats water which evaporates and rises. High up it cools and condenses around tiny dust particles forming clouds. When droplets combine and grow heavy enough gravity pulls them down as rain. The water you drink may have once been a dinosaur's puddle.

Try It Yourself

Put a cold glass outside on a humid day. Watch droplets form on the outside — condensation, the same process that forms clouds and starts the rain cycle.

Ask This Next

Why do rivers always reach the sea? → #53

#46 Why Do Volcanoes Erupt?

Quick Answer

Volcanoes erupt when magma builds enough pressure underground to burst through weak points in Earth's crust — like squeezing a toothpaste tube until it pops.

Let's Go Deeper

Earth's crust is made of tectonic plates constantly moving. Where plates collide or pull apart, magma forces its way up. Once it reaches the surface it's called lava. Some eruptions are slow lava flows. Others are explosive blasts of ash and gas traveling at 700 km/h.

Try It Yourself

Mix baking soda and vinegar in a tall bottle — CO2 pressure builds and erupts. Real volcanoes work similarly — dissolved gases expand rapidly as pressure drops.

Ask This Next

Why do earthquakes happen? → #49

#47 Why Do Leaves Change Color in Autumn?

Quick Answer

Leaves hide yellow and orange pigments beneath green chlorophyll all year. In autumn shorter days trigger chlorophyll breakdown, revealing the hidden colors before leaves drop.

Let's Go Deeper

Chlorophyll captures sunlight for photosynthesis and breaks down in autumn as trees shed leaves to conserve water. Yellow carotenoids were hidden all along. Red anthocyanins are newly made as the tree recycles nutrients before dropping leaves.

Try It Yourself

Tear a leaf into a jar of rubbing alcohol. Dip a filter strip in the liquid and leave to dry. You will see green and yellow pigments separate — the hidden colors were there all along.

Ask This Next

Why do plants need sunlight? → #51

#48 Why Is the Ocean Salty?

Quick Answer

Rain dissolves salt minerals from rocks and carries them to the sea via rivers. Water evaporates but salt stays behind. Over billions of years the salt has accumulated.

Let's Go Deeper

Rivers carry about 4 billion tonnes of dissolved salts to the oceans every year. The ocean has been collecting this for 3.8 billion years. Underwater volcanic vents also release minerals directly into the sea. If all the ocean water evaporated the salt left behind would cover every continent 150 metres deep.

Try It Yourself

Fill a shallow dish with salty water and leave in the sun for a day. Water evaporates but salt crystals remain — exactly how ocean salt concentrates over.

Ask This Next

Why do rivers always reach the sea? → #53

#49 Why Do Earthquakes Happen?

Quick Answer

Earth's crust is made of giant plates slowly moving. When plates grind together and suddenly slip, they release enormous stored energy as seismic waves that shake everything above.

Let's Go Deeper

Tectonic plates move at fingernail-growth speed but lock at edges building stress for centuries before releasing all at once. The 2011 Japan earthquake shifted Earth's axis by 17cm and shortened the day by 1.8 microseconds.

Try It Yourself

Press two books together side-by-side and push them toward each other. Let one slip suddenly — it jumps. That sudden energy release is exactly what an earthquake does.

Ask This Next

Why do volcanoes erupt? → #46

#50 Why Does the Wind Blow?

Quick Answer

Wind is air moving from high pressure to low pressure. The sun heats the ground unevenly — warm air rises creating low pressure, cool air rushes in to fill the gap.

Let's Go Deeper

The sun heats the equator more than the poles, creating giant global wind circulation patterns. Earth's rotation also bends wind paths — called the Coriolis effect. This is why storms spin clockwise in the southern hemisphere and anticlockwise in the northern hemisphere.

Try It Yourself

Hold your hand over a warm radiator — feel air rising. Hold it to the side — feel cooler air rushing in to replace it. That small current drives every wind on Earth from a gentle breeze to a hurricane.

Ask This Next

Why does thunder follow lightning? → #55

#51 Why Do Plants Need Sunlight?

Quick Answer

Plants use sunlight as energy to convert water and carbon dioxide into sugar — their food. This process called photosynthesis also produces the oxygen we breathe as a byproduct.

Let's Go Deeper

Chlorophyll molecules inside leaf cells capture light energy and use it to split water molecules. The hydrogen combines with CO2 to make glucose sugar. The leftover oxygen is released into the air. Every breath you take contains oxygen made by a plant doing exactly this process.

Try It Yourself

Put a plant in a dark cupboard for three days. Compare its leaves with one left in sunlight. The dark plant yellows as chlorophyll breaks down without light.

Ask This Next

Why do leaves change color in autumn? → #47

#52 Why Do Flowers Have a Smell?

Quick Answer

Flowers smell to attract pollinators like bees and moths. The scent advertises nectar inside. Without pollinators visiting, flowers cannot reproduce — it is survival advertising.

Let's Go Deeper

Different flowers evolved scents to attract specific pollinators. Night flowers are white and strongly scented to attract moths in the dark. Some smell like rotting meat to attract flies. Scent comes from volatile compounds evaporating from petals — warmth increases the smell.

Try It Yourself

Smell the same flower in the morning and at midday on a warm day. It will smell stronger when warmer as more scent compounds evaporate.

Ask This Next

Why do plants need sunlight? → #51

#53 Why Do Rivers Always Reach the Sea?

Quick Answer

Water always flows downhill following gravity. It takes the path of least resistance — finding cracks and valleys until it reaches the lowest point possible.

Let's Go Deeper

Gravity pulls water downward at 9.8 m/s^2. Rivers carve their own channels — soft rock erodes faster creating bends. The Nile travels over 6,600km before reaching the sea but gravity always wins eventually.

Try It Yourself

Pour water onto a sloped sand tray. Watch it carve its own channel finding the lowest path. Add obstacles and see how it flows around them.

Ask This Next

Why is the ocean salty? → #48

#54 Why Do Deserts Exist?

Quick Answer

Deserts form where air descends and warms, evaporating moisture before rain can fall. Most deserts sit at 30 degrees latitude where global wind patterns cause dry air to sink.

Let's Go Deeper

Hot air rises at the equator, drops rain in tropical forests, then spreads toward the poles. At 30 degrees it descends as dry warm air that absorbs moisture. Mountains also create deserts by blocking rain — a rain shadow. Antarctica is Earth's largest desert.

Try It Yourself

Hold a hairdryer on warm setting over your wet hand. Moving warm air evaporates water rapidly. That is what descending desert air does — moisture evaporates.

Ask This Next

Why does the wind blow? → #50

#55 Why Does Thunder Follow Lightning?

Quick Answer

Lightning and thunder happen at the same time but light travels near-instantly. Sound takes about 3 seconds per kilometre to reach you.

Let's Go Deeper

Light travels at 300,000 km per second — effectively instant. Sound travels at 343 metres per second. Count the seconds between flash and thunder and divide by 3 to find how many kilometres away the storm is. Lightning bolt temperatures reach 30,000 Kelvin — five times hotter than the sun's surface.

Try It Yourself

Next thunderstorm count seconds between flash and thunder and divide by 3. That is the distance in kilometres. Watch the gap shrink as the storm approaches.

Ask This Next

Why does lightning strike tall things? → #57

#56 Why Do Rivers Carve Canyons?

⚡ **Quick Answer**

Rivers carry rock particles that grind away the riverbed like sandpaper. Over millions of years this erosion cuts deeper into the earth — the Grand Canyon took 5-6 million years.

Let's Go Deeper

The Colorado River carries 400,000 tonnes of sediment daily, abrading rock below. Softer layers erode faster creating steps. The Grand Canyon is 1.6km deep exposing rock 2 billion years old — almost half Earth's age.

Try It Yourself

Pour water steadily over a sand pile for several minutes. Watch it carve a channel growing deeper over time. Add pebbles to see how sediment does the cutting.

? Ask This Next

Why does it rain? → #45

#57 Why Does Lightning Strike Tall Things?

⚡ Quick Answer

Lightning takes the path of least resistance from cloud to ground. Tall objects are closer to the cloud and send stronger upward streamers — making them the easiest connection.

Let's Go Deeper

A lightning bolt is a stepped leader reaching down from the cloud meeting a return stroke shooting up from the ground. They meet in the middle. Taller objects send stronger streamers that connect first. Lightning rods provide a safe controlled path to ground.

Try It Yourself

Rub a balloon on your hair and bring it near small paper pieces. Paper jumps upward — positive charges attracted to the negatively charged balloon.

? Ask This Next

Why can quicksand trap you? → #58

#58 Why Can Quicksand Trap You?

⚡ Quick Answer

Quicksand is a non-Newtonian fluid — liquid when still but solid when you move suddenly. Panicking makes it grip tighter. Moving slowly and horizontally lets you float free.

Let's Go Deeper

Quicksand is sand saturated with water that has lost structural friction. Sudden force causes particles to lock together — harder you push the more solid it becomes. Human density is less than quicksand so you cannot fully sink, but suction forces can be enormous.

Try It Yourself

Mix cornstarch and water until thick. Punch it quickly — feels solid. Press slowly — finger sinks through like liquid. Try pulling your finger out slowly.

? Ask This Next

Why do some plants eat insects? → #59

#59 Why Do Some Plants Eat Insects?

Quick Answer

Carnivorous plants evolved in nitrogen-poor soils. They trap insects to absorb the nitrogen they cannot get from the soil — a clever evolutionary workaround for a very difficult environment.

Let's Go Deeper

The Venus flytrap snaps in under 100 milliseconds when trigger hairs are touched twice — the two-touch rule prevents wasting energy on raindrops. Pitcher plants use slippery surfaces and enzymes. Sundews use sticky mucilage. All evolved independently facing the same soil problem.

Try It Yourself

Touch one Venus flytrap trigger hair — nothing happens. Touch it again quickly — it snaps. The two-touch system prevents false triggers from raindrops.

Ask This Next

Why does the sea have waves? → #60

#60 Why Does the Sea Have Waves?

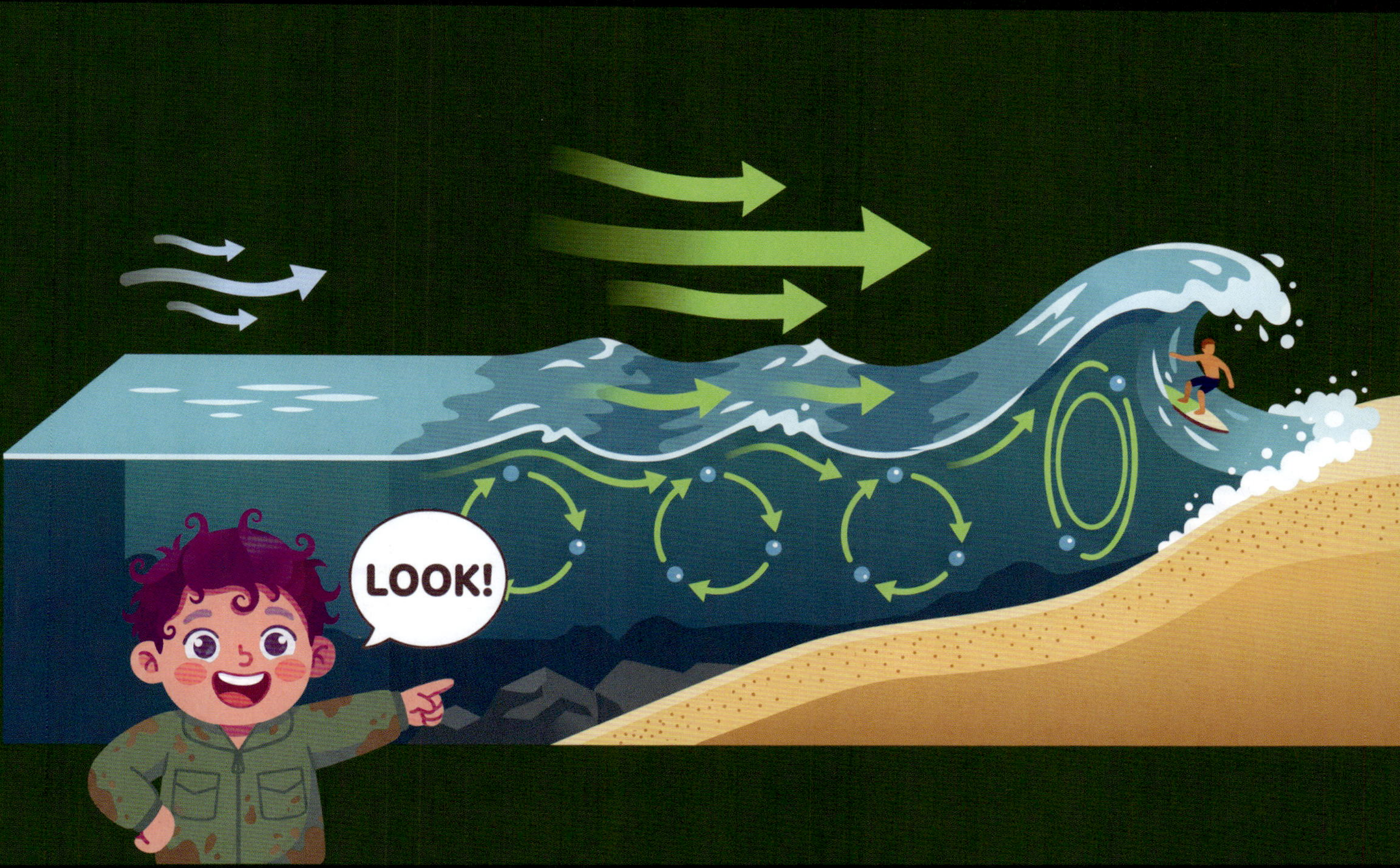

Quick Answer

Waves are energy moving through water, not water moving forward. Wind transfers energy to the ocean surface creating ripples that grow into waves. The water itself mostly moves in circles.

Let's Go Deeper

Wind creates friction that transfers energy into the water surface. Water molecules move in circular orbits — rising on the wave face, forward at the crest, falling behind, backward in the trough. As waves approach a beach the seabed slows the bottom while the top keeps moving, causing it to topple and break.

Try It Yourself

Float a cork in a bowl and blow gently across the surface creating ripples. Watch the cork bob up and down in place rather than traveling with the wave. Waves move through water.

Ask This Next

Why do rivers carve canyons? → #56

Chapter 5

Everyday Science

Have you ever wondered why stepping on a Lego hurts so much, why glue doesn't stick to the inside of its own bottle, or why your voice sounds so weird in a recording? In this chapter we explore 14 of the most surprising questions about the ordinary objects and forces around you every single day.

In this chapter:

#61 Why Does Ice Melt?

⚡ Quick Answer

Ice melts when heat energy breaks the bonds holding water molecules in a rigid lattice. The molecules absorb enough energy to move freely past each other and become liquid water.

Let's Go Deeper

In ice molecules vibrate in fixed positions locked by hydrogen bonds. Add heat and they vibrate faster until bonds break and molecules slide freely — that is melting. At 100 degrees they escape as steam.

Try It Yourself

Put identical ice cubes on a metal tray and a wooden board. The metal cube melts much faster — metal conducts room heat into ice more efficiently than wood.

? Ask This Next

Why does metal feel colder than wood? → #65

#62 Why Do Magnets Attract and Repel?

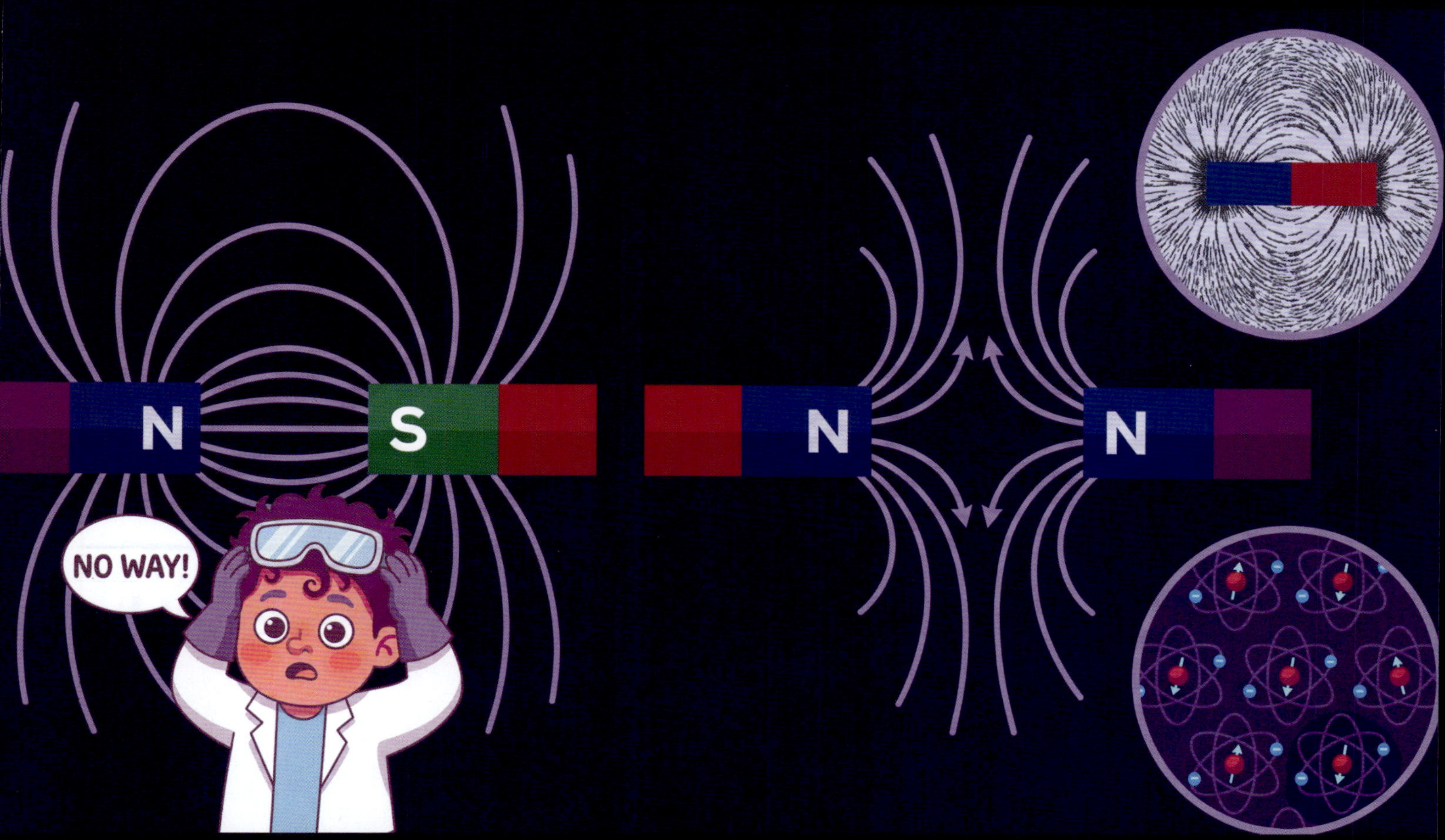

Quick Answer

Opposite magnetic poles create field lines that pull toward each other. Same poles repel because their field lines clash. This force comes from electrons spinning in alignment.

Let's Go Deeper

In most materials electrons spin randomly and cancel out. In ferromagnetic materials like iron, electron groups align creating magnetic domains. When all domains point the same way you have a magnet. Opposite poles attract because their field lines flow together smoothly.

Try It Yourself

Scatter iron filings on paper and hold a magnet underneath. The filings reveal the invisible field line pattern. Now try two magnets attracting and repelling.

Ask This Next

Why does electricity make light? → #71

#63 Why Does Soap Make Bubbles?

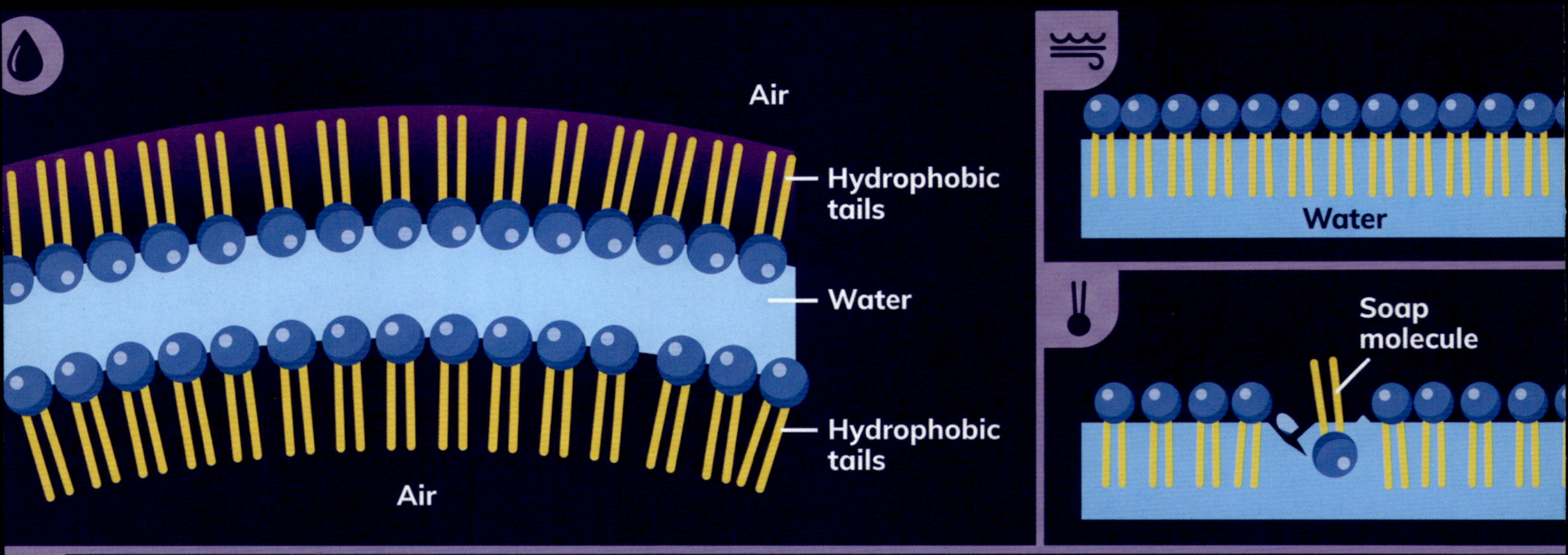

Quick Answer

Soap reduces water's surface tension allowing it to stretch into a thin elastic film. Soap molecules form two layers trapping water between them. Air pressure inside keeps the bubble inflated.

Let's Go Deeper

Water molecules pull strongly toward each other creating surface tension. Soap molecules wedge between water molecules spacing them apart and reducing tension allowing water to stretch into a film. Spheres have the smallest surface area for a given volume — the minimum energy shape.

Try It Yourself

Touch a soap bubble with a wet finger — it does not pop. Touch with a dry finger — it pops instantly. Dry surfaces break the soap film. The bubble wall is extremely delicate.

Ask This Next

Why do mirrors show everything backwards? → #72

#64 Why Do Things Fall Down?

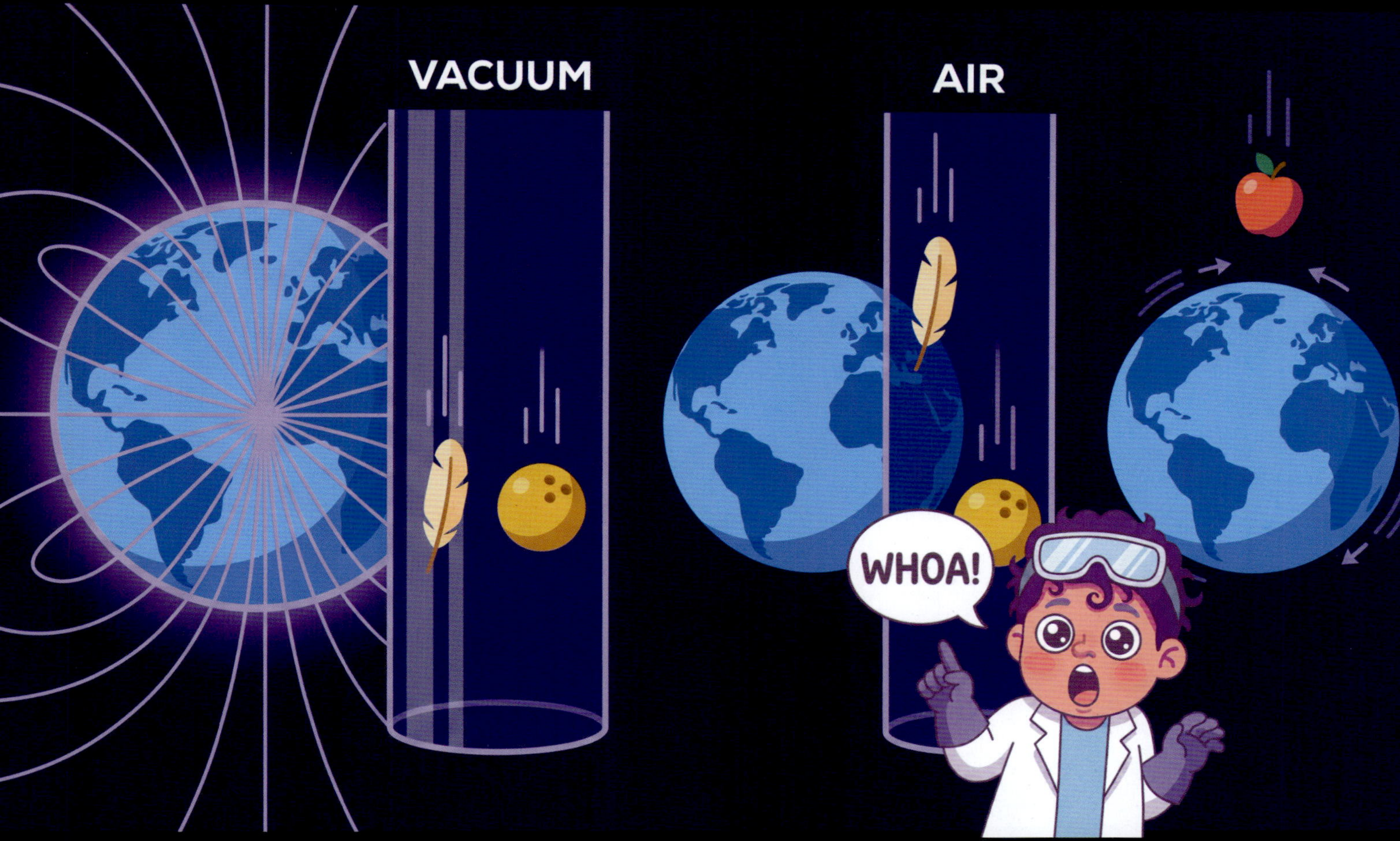

⚡ Quick Answer

Gravity is attraction between all objects with mass. Earth is so massive it pulls everything toward its center. In a vacuum all objects fall at the same rate regardless of weight.

Let's Go Deeper

Earth's mass creates a gravitational field attracting everything toward its center at 9.8 m/s^2 regardless of weight. In a vacuum without air resistance a feather and a hammer fall identically — proved on the Moon during Apollo 15.

Try It Yourself

Drop a heavy book and paper simultaneously. Paper floats slowly due to air resistance. Place paper on top of the book and drop together — the book pushes air out of the way.

? Ask This Next

Why does metal feel colder than wood? → #65

#65 Why Does Metal Feel Colder Than Wood?

⚡ Quick Answer

Metal and wood in the same room are the same temperature. Metal feels colder because it conducts heat from your hand much faster — your skin loses heat quickly and your brain interprets cold.

Let's Go Deeper

Your skin senses temperature by detecting how fast heat moves. Metal has free electrons that transfer heat rapidly. Wood barely conducts heat at all — why wooden pot handles stay cool. Your perception of cold is actually your body detecting rapid heat loss not actual coldness.

Try It Yourself

Leave a metal spoon and wooden spoon in the same spot for 30 minutes. Touch both — they feel different. Measure both with a thermometer — they are identical.

? Ask This Next

Why does ice melt? → #61

#66 Why Does a Rainbow Appear After Rain?

⚡ Quick Answer

Raindrops act as tiny prisms — sunlight enters, bends, reflects off the inside, bends again as it exits, separating into colors. You see a rainbow when the sun is behind you and rain ahead.

Let's Go Deeper

White light contains all colors traveling at slightly different speeds. When light enters water it slows and bends at different angles per color — refraction — separating into the spectrum. Each raindrop sends a different color to your eye depending on its angle. No two people see exactly the same rainbow.

Try It Yourself

Stand with your back to the sun and spray water from a hose in front of you. You will create your own rainbow. Mist droplets refract and separate sunlight into visible colors.

? Ask This Next

Why doesn't glue stick to its own bottle?

→ #73

#67 Why Does Wood Float But Metal Sink?

Quick Answer

Objects float when less dense than water. Wood is less dense so it floats. Metal is denser so it sinks. But a hollow metal ship floats because its overall density including air is lower than water.

Let's Go Deeper

Density is mass divided by volume. Wood has air pockets making it less dense than water. Steel is eight times denser than water. But a steel ship displaces a volume of water weighing more than the ship itself so it floats. Melted into a ball it would sink instantly.

Try It Yourself

Roll modelling clay into a ball — it sinks. Reshape the same clay into a shallow bowl — it floats. Same material, different shape displaces more water than the solid ball.

Ask This Next

Why does soap make bubbles? → #63

#68 Why Does Music Make You Feel Things?

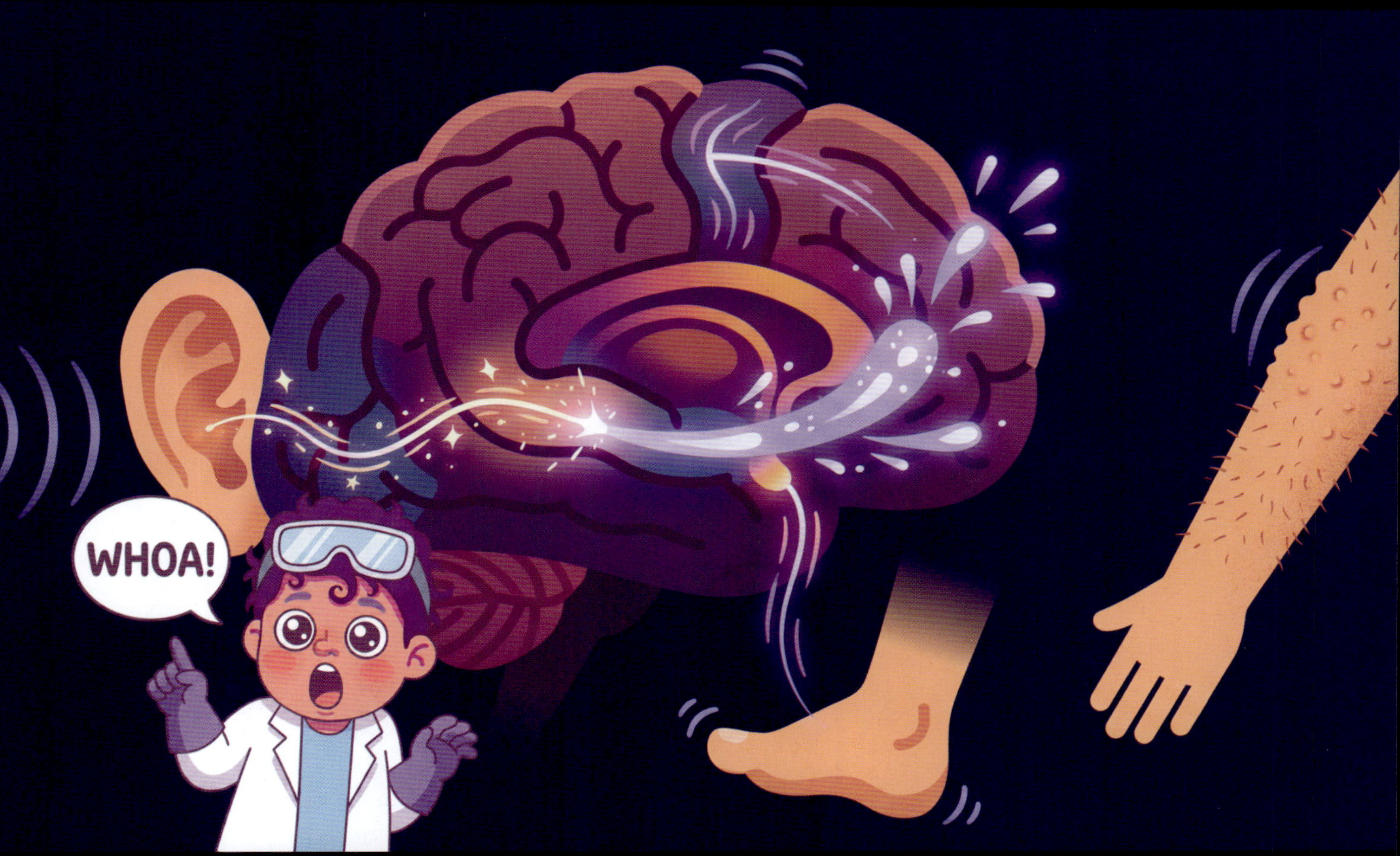

⚡ Quick Answer

Music triggers dopamine release in the brain's reward system — the same chemical released by food and love. It also activates the motor cortex causing movement and the limbic system controlling emotion.

Let's Go Deeper

Rhythm activates motor areas causing movement. Melody activates emotional memory. Unexpected chord changes cause dopamine surges — the musical surprise reward. About two thirds of people experience frisson — goosebumps from music — correlating with higher openness to experience.

Try It Yourself

Listen to music that gives you chills. Notice which moment triggers the feeling — a key change, a build, an instrument entering. That is your dopamine response activating.

? Ask This Next

Why does fire need oxygen to burn? → #69

#69 Why Does Fire Need Oxygen to Burn?

Quick Answer

Burning is a chemical reaction between fuel and oxygen releasing heat and light. Without oxygen the reaction cannot happen. Remove heat, fuel or oxygen and fire immediately dies.

Let's Go Deeper

Combustion breaks fuel molecules apart and recombines them with oxygen, releasing energy. Carbon and hydrogen produce carbon dioxide and water vapor plus heat and light. Fire extinguishers work by removing one of the three requirements: cooling removes heat, CO2 displaces oxygen, foam smothers fuel.

Try It Yourself

Lower a glass jar over a candle without sealing the base. The flame shrinks and dies as oxygen is consumed. Lift the jar and it relights from the still-hot wick vapor.

Ask This Next

Why does electricity make light? → #71

#70 Why Do Shadows Change Size?

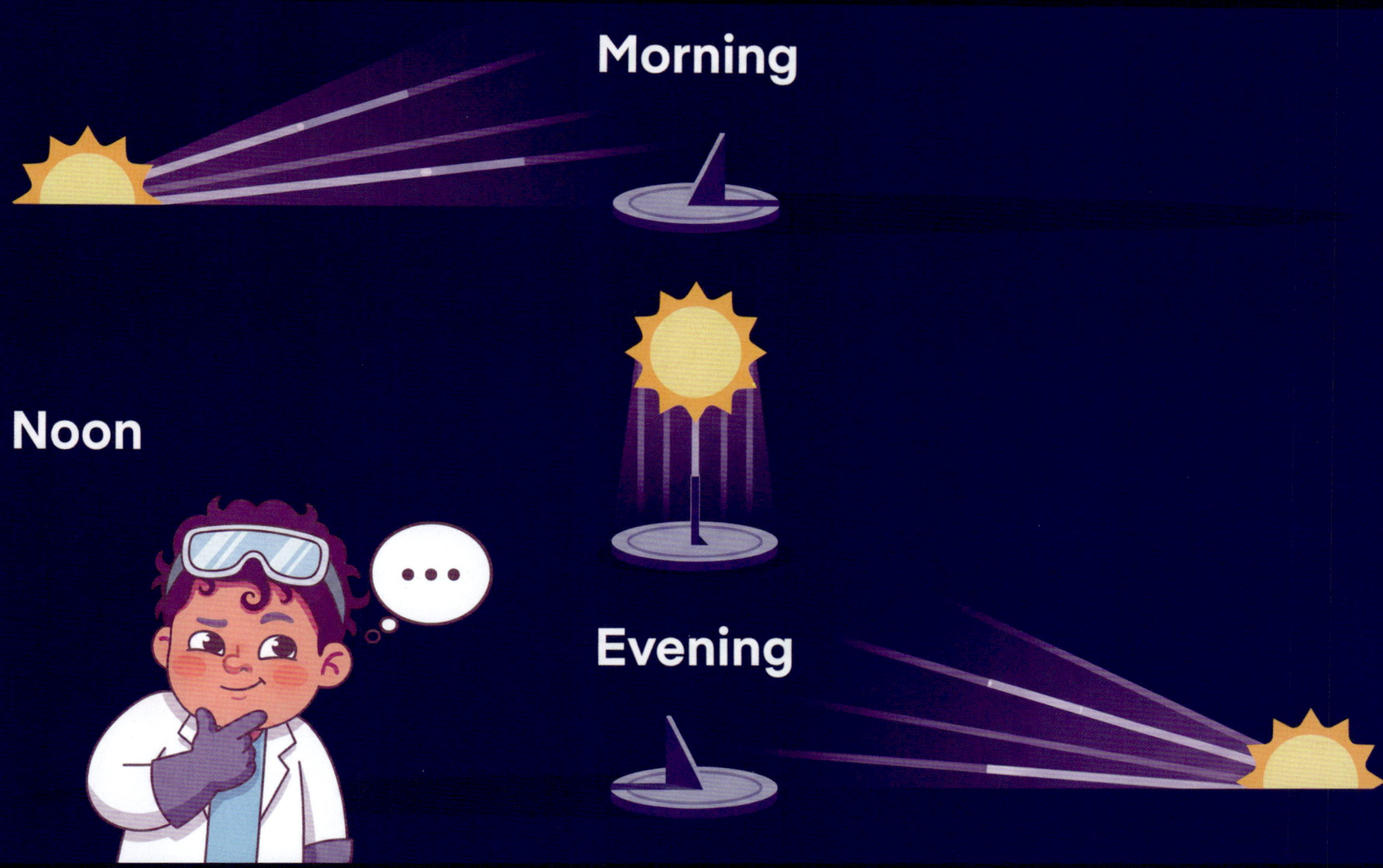

Quick Answer

Shadows form where an object blocks light. When the sun is low the light hits at a shallow angle and the shadow stretches long. When the sun is overhead the shadow is directly beneath you.

Let's Go Deeper

A shadow is simply an absence of light. Its length depends on the angle between light source and object. Ancient Egyptians used shadow lengths to calculate building heights and Greeks used them to estimate Earth's circumference.

Try It Yourself

Trace your shadow on pavement with chalk at morning, noon and afternoon. Compare the lengths and directions. Then build a sundial by sticking a pencil upright in the ground.

Ask This Next

Why does music make you feel things? → #68

#71 Why Does Electricity Make Light?

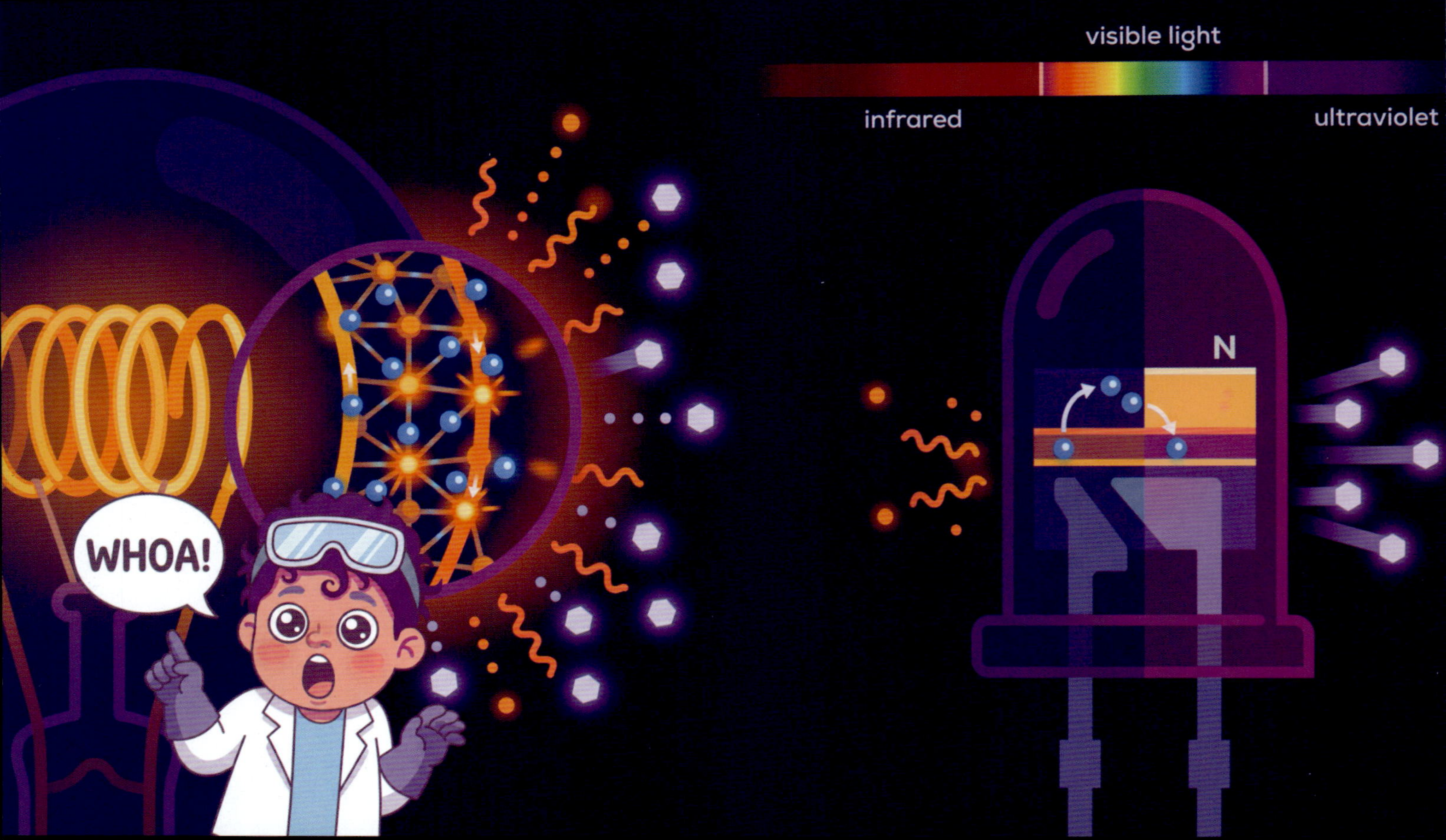

Quick Answer
Electricity forces electrons through resistance. Collisions release energy as heat and light. In LEDs electrons jump between energy levels releasing that energy directly as visible light.

Let's Go Deeper
In an incandescent bulb the filament heats to 2,500 degrees Celsius — so hot it glows. But 95% of the energy becomes heat not light. LEDs release energy directly as photons — far more efficient. LED color is determined by the energy gap in the semiconductor material.

Try It Yourself
Hold your hand near a lit incandescent bulb — feel the heat. Hold it near an LED of the same brightness — barely warm. Both make the same light but the LED wastes less energy.

Ask This Next
Why do magnets attract and repel? → #62

#72 Why Do Mirrors Show Everything Backwards?

Quick Answer

Mirrors reverse front and back not left and right. You appear reversed because you mentally rotate yourself to face you. Lay a book on a mirror and text flips upside down not backward sideways.

Let's Go Deeper

A mirror reflects light at equal angles. The reversal you see is depth reversal — your nose stays closest but you perceive it as left-right reversal because you imagine walking around to face yourself which would flip left and right.

Try It Yourself

Write a word on paper and hold it face-down against a mirror — text appears backwards because the paper is front-to-back reversed. Hold text against a window and read outside.

Ask This Next

Why doesn't glue stick to its own bottle? → #73

#73 Why Doesn't Glue Stick to Its Own Bottle?

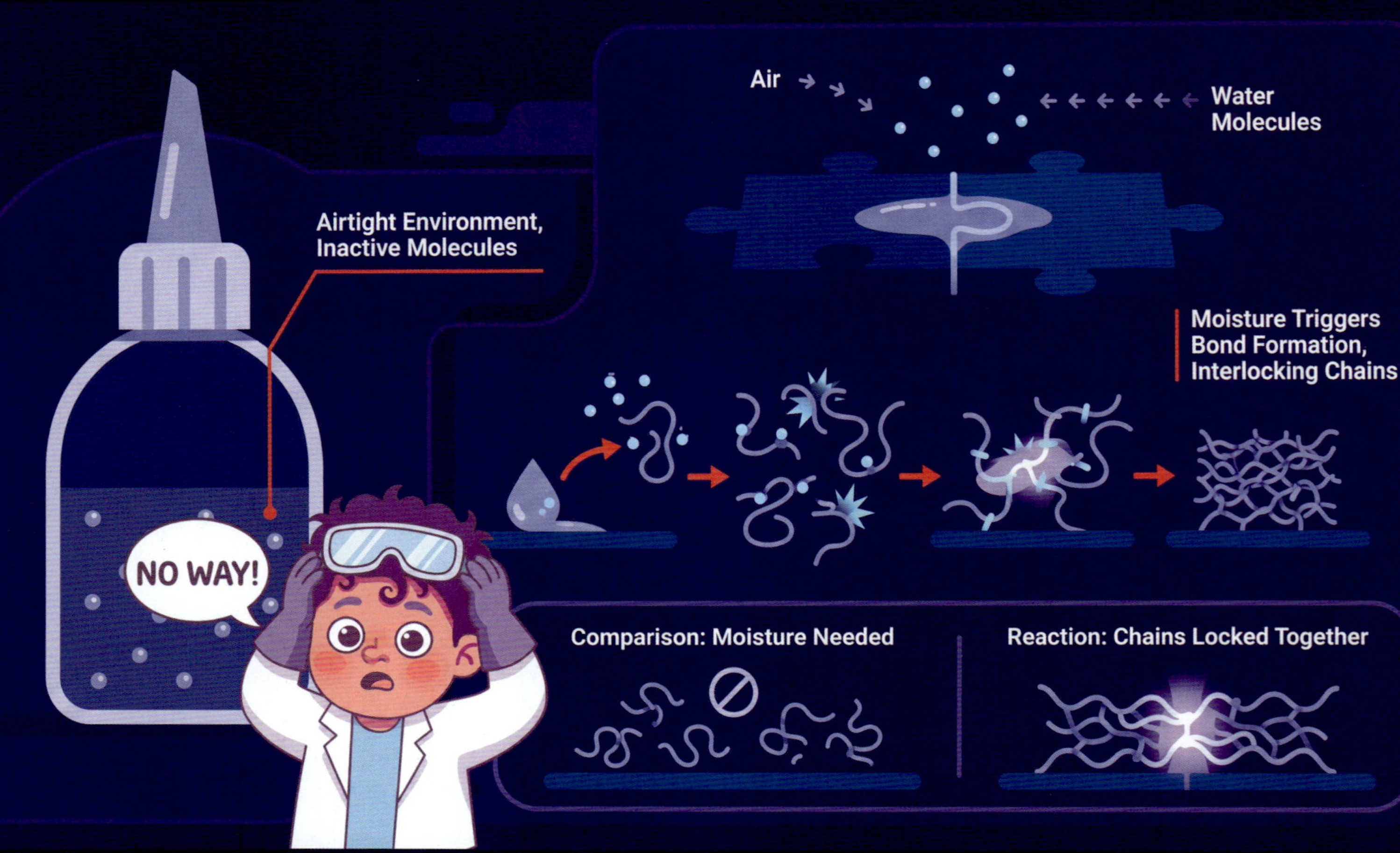

⚡ Quick Answer

Glue needs air or moisture to activate and set. Inside a sealed bottle there is no air or moisture so it stays liquid. The bottle is designed to keep the activating trigger away from the glue.

Let's Go Deeper

PVA glue hardens as water evaporates. Super glue is triggered by moisture — even the thin layer on your skin. Inside an airtight bottle there is no evaporation or moisture to trigger the reaction so it stays permanently liquid until exposed.

Try It Yourself

Leave a blob of PVA glue on paper — note how long it takes to dry. Put a blob under a glass trapping the air — it stays wet much longer. No air circulation slows evaporation.

? Ask This Next

Why does stepping on a Lego hurt so much?
→ #74

#74 Why Does Stepping on a Lego Hurt So Much?

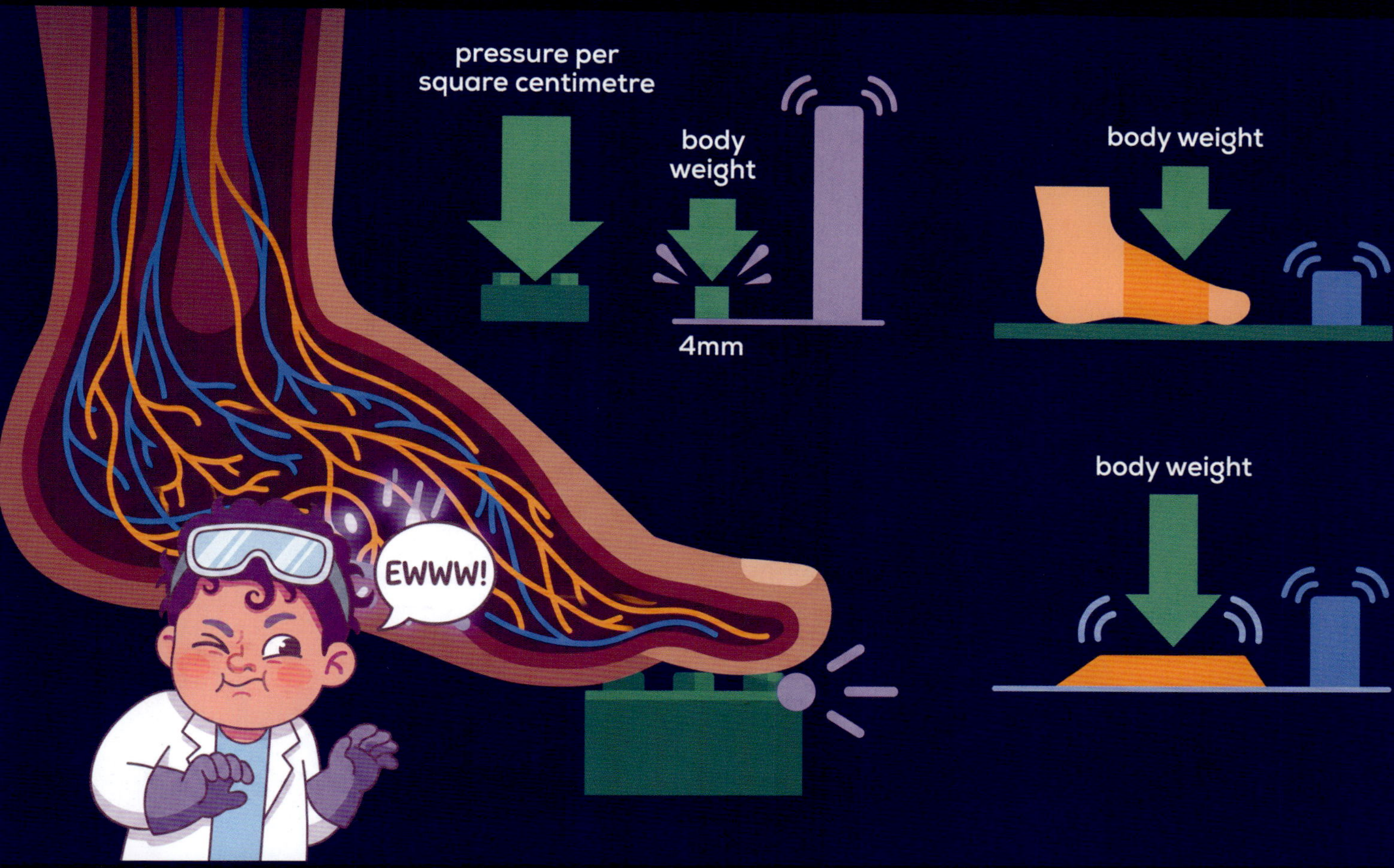

Quick Answer

Your full body weight concentrates onto a tiny hard Lego corner. The foot arch has dense nerve endings for balance. Enormous pressure on a highly sensitive area creates very sharp pain.

Let's Go Deeper

Pressure equals force divided by area. Your body weight spread across a flat floor is harmless. The same force on a 4mm Lego corner creates about 30,000 Newtons per square metre — triggering every pain receptor in your foot arch simultaneously.

Try It Yourself

Press a pencil eraser against your arm — comfortable. Flip it and press the sharp tip with the same force — much more intense. Same force, smaller area, higher pressure.

Ask This Next

Why does soap make bubbles? → #63

Chapter 6

Food & Taste

Have you ever wondered why onions make you cry, why eating ice cream too fast gives you a headache, or what is actually growing on food that's gone bad? In this chapter we explore 12 of the most delicious — and occasionally revolting — questions about food, taste and what happens inside your body when you eat.

In this chapter:

#75 Why Do We Get Hungry?

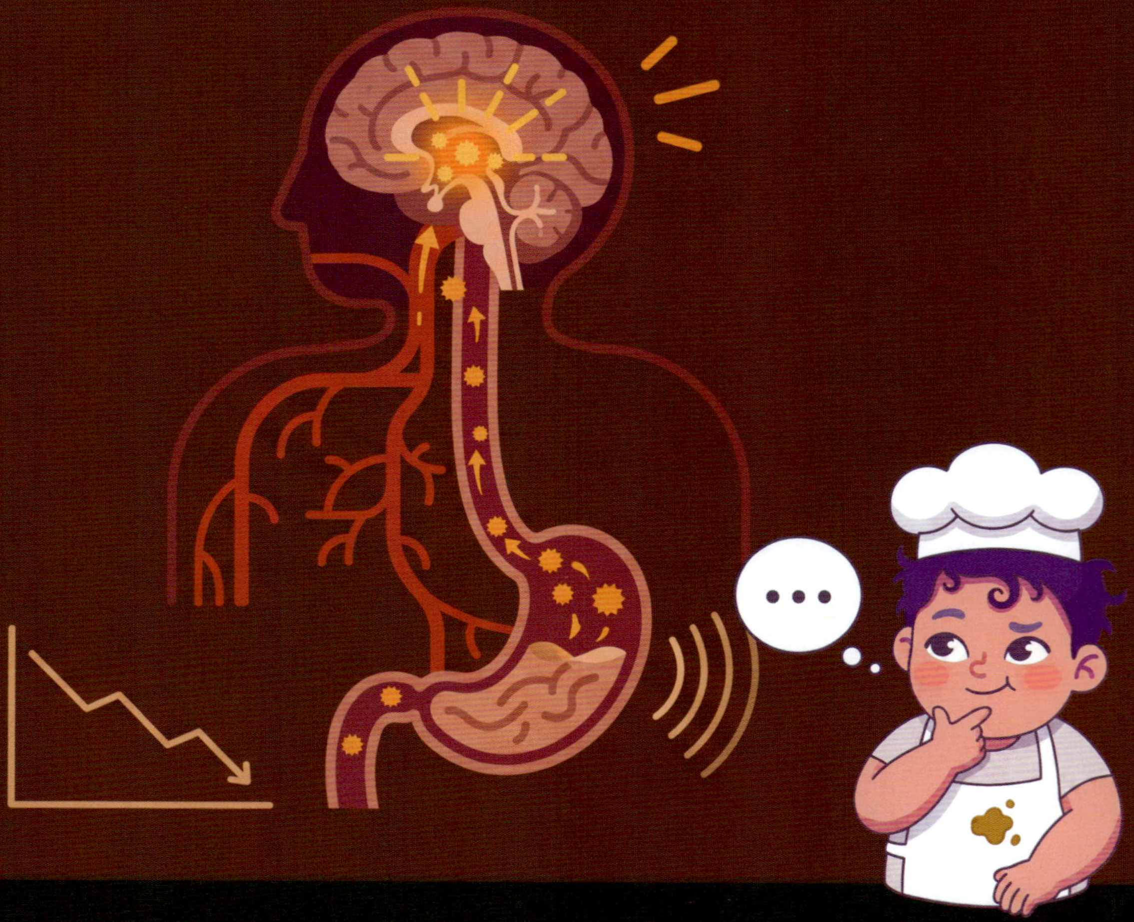

Quick Answer

When your stomach empties it releases a hormone called ghrelin into your blood. Ghrelin travels to your brain and triggers the hunger signal. Your blood sugar dropping also tells your brain to eat.

Let's Go Deeper

Hunger is a complex hormone orchestra. Ghrelin rises before meals and falls after eating. Leptin from fat cells signals fullness. The hypothalamus in your brain monitors both and decides when to send hunger signals. It takes about 20 minutes after eating for fullness signals to reach the brain — which is why overeating happens easily.

Try It Yourself

Notice your hunger level every hour for a day and write it down with the time. You will likely see a pattern — hunger peaks roughly every 3-4 hours as ghrelin levels rise.

Ask This Next

Why does your stomach growl in public? → #80

#76 Why Does Bread Rise?

Quick Answer

Yeast are tiny living organisms that eat sugar in the dough and produce CO2 gas as waste. The gas gets trapped in the stretchy gluten network and inflates the dough like millions of tiny balloons.

Let's Go Deeper

Yeast is a single-celled fungus that has been used in baking for at least 5,000 years. It feeds on sugars through fermentation producing CO2 and alcohol — the alcohol evaporates in the oven. The gluten protein network in wheat flour forms an elastic mesh that traps the gas bubbles. Heat kills the yeast and hardens the bread.

Try It Yourself

Mix a teaspoon of yeast with warm water and a pinch of sugar in a bottle. Stretch a balloon over the neck. Within 15 minutes the balloon inflates as yeast produces CO2 gas.

Ask This Next

Why does chocolate make you feel happy?
→ #84

#77 Why Does Food Taste Different With a Cold?

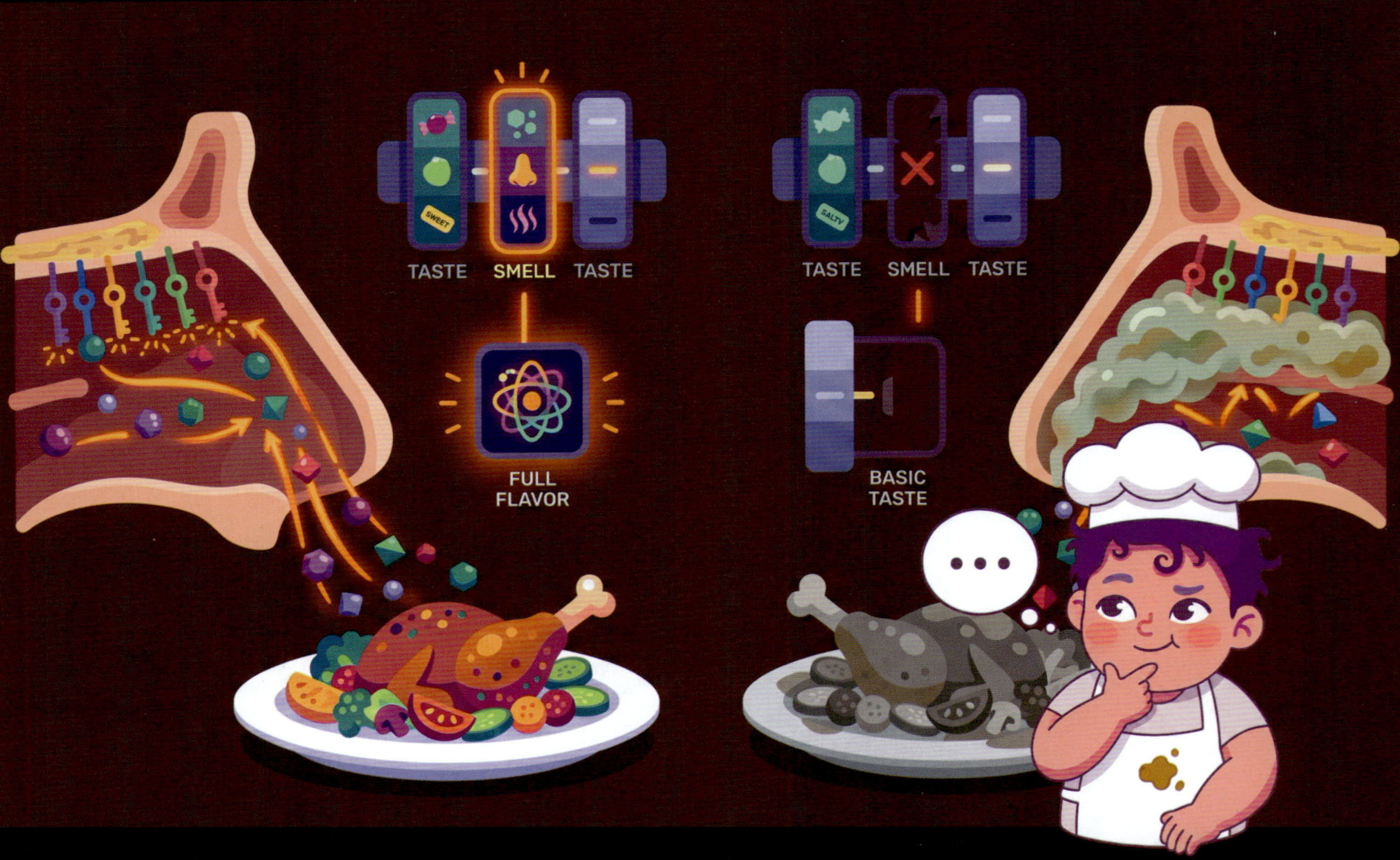

Quick Answer

About 80% of what you taste is actually smell. Your nose detects flavors through the back of your throat while you chew. A blocked nose cuts off this signal leaving only the five basic tastes.

Let's Go Deeper

Your tongue only detects five basic tastes — sweet, sour, salty, bitter and umami. Everything else — the difference between strawberry and raspberry, coffee and chocolate — is smell detected retronasally as you chew. This is why pinching your nose makes food almost tasteless. Smell and taste signals combine inside the brain.

Try It Yourself

Pinch your nose closed and eat small pieces of apple and raw potato alternately. Without smell they are almost indistinguishable — both just taste slightly sweet and crunchy.

Ask This Next

Why does your mouth water when you smell food? → #78

#78 Why Does Your Mouth Water When You Smell Food?

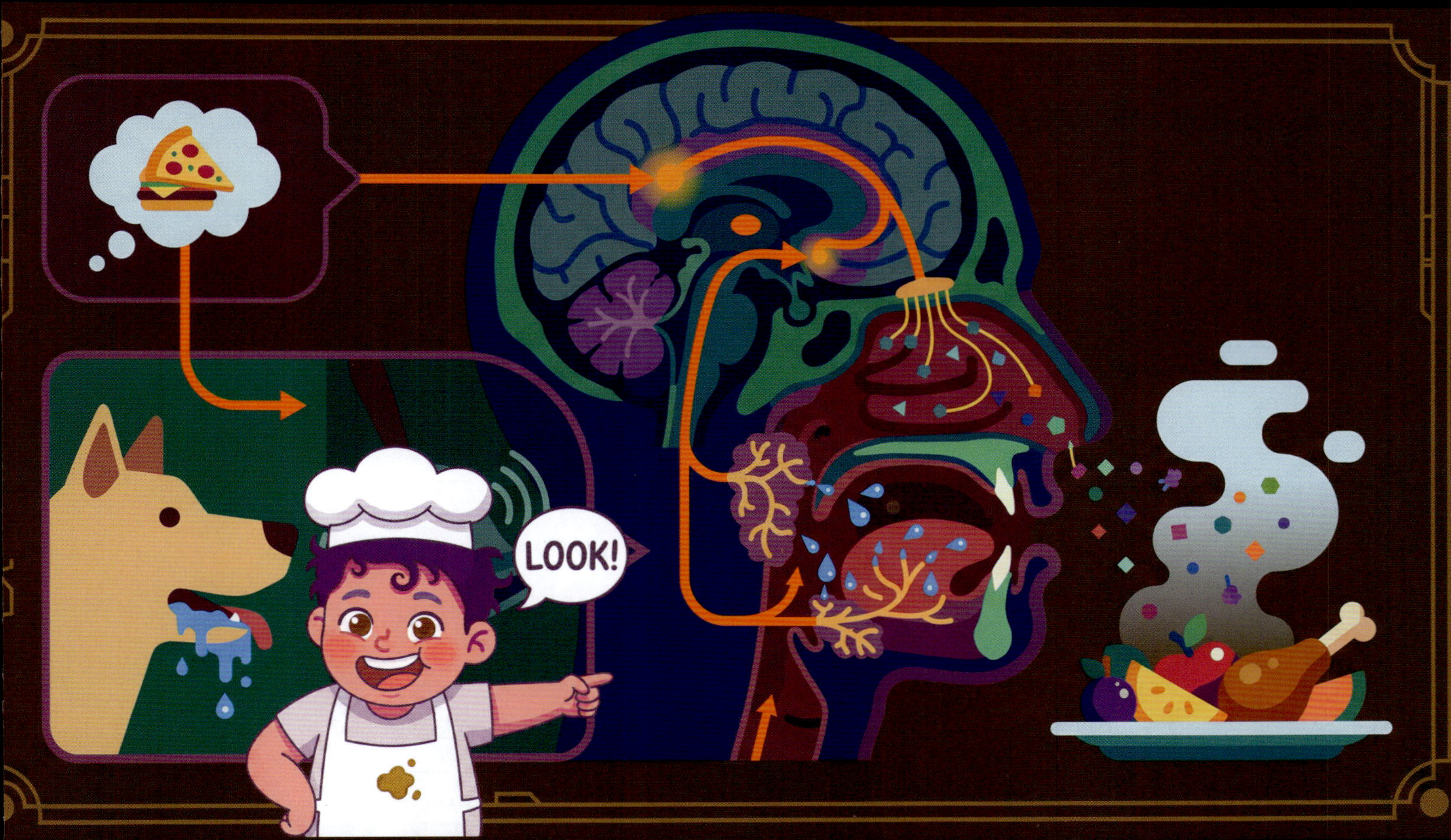

Quick Answer

Smelling food sends a signal to your brain which immediately activates your salivary glands. Saliva starts digestion before food even enters your mouth — dissolving flavor molecules for tasting.

Let's Go Deeper

This is a Pavlovian reflex — your brain has learned that smell means food is coming. Saliva contains amylase enzymes that begin breaking down starch immediately. It also dissolves flavor compounds so they reach your taste receptors. Even imagining food triggers the same response — your salivary glands activate automatically.

Try It Yourself

Think vividly about your favorite food for 30 seconds — imagine cutting it, smelling it and eating it in detail. Notice your mouth beginning to water. Your brain triggered salivation.

Ask This Next

Why do we get hungry? → #75

#79 Why Do Some People Love Spicy Food?

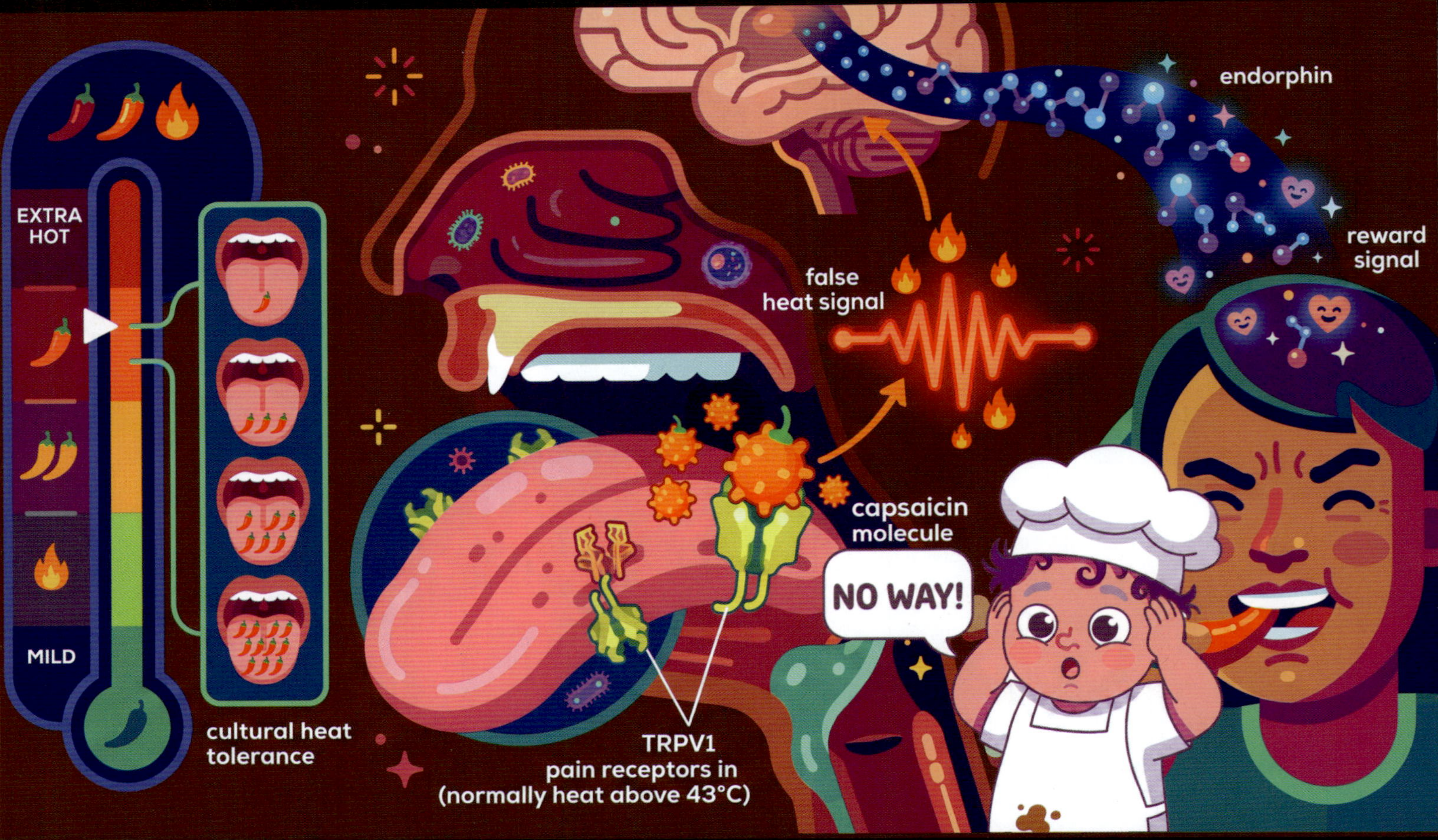

Quick Answer

Spicy food triggers pain receptors in your mouth that normally detect heat. Your brain responds to this false fire alarm by releasing endorphins — pleasure chemicals. Spice lovers begin craving that rush.

Let's Go Deeper

Capsaicin in chilis binds to TRPV1 receptors that normally detect temperatures above 43 degrees. Your brain cannot tell the difference between real heat and capsaicin — it releases endorphins either way. Repeated exposure desensitizes the receptors explaining why spice tolerance increases. Capsaicin also triggers sweating reflexes.

Try It Yourself

After eating something mildly spicy drink water — barely helps. Drink cold milk — much better relief. Capsaicin is oil-based and not water soluble. Milk breaks it down.

? Ask This Next

Why does food taste different with a cold?
→ #77

#80 Why Does Your Stomach Growl in Public?

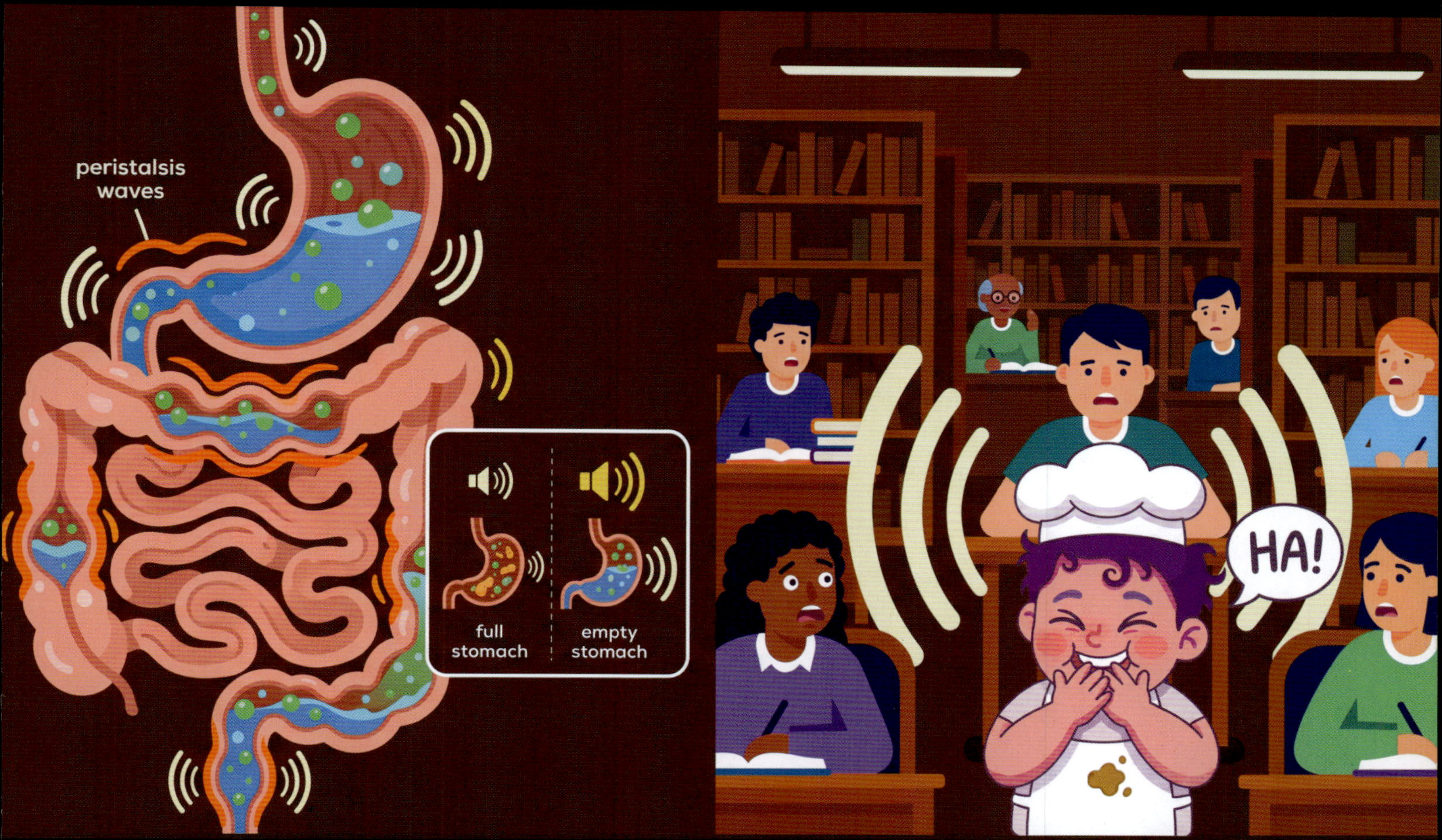

Quick Answer

Your digestive system constantly contracts and squeezes to move food along — called peristalsis. When your stomach is empty these contractions move air and liquid making the growling sound.

Let's Go Deeper

Peristalsis happens continuously even when you are not eating — the digestive system clears itself every few hours in a process called the migrating motor complex. The growling sound occurs when these contractions move gas and liquid through the stomach and intestines. An empty stomach amplifies the sound like an echo chamber.

Try It Yourself

Place a stethoscope or just your ear against your own stomach when hungry and wait quietly. You will hear gurgles, rumbles and liquid sounds — your digestive system working continuously.

Ask This Next

Why do we get hungry? → #75

#81 Why Does Onion Make You Cry But Not Garlic?

Quick Answer

Cutting onions releases a volatile sulfur gas called syn-propanethial-S-oxide which floats upward and irritates your eyes causing tears. Garlic has similar sulfur compounds but in lower concentrations.

Let's Go Deeper

Onion cells store sulfur compounds and enzymes separately. Cutting breaks cells mixing them together, triggering a chemical reaction that produces the volatile lachrymatory agent. It evolved as a defense against animals eating the bulb. Chilling onions before cutting slows the reaction and reduces crying.

Try It Yourself

Cut one onion at room temperature and one straight from the fridge. The cold onion produces significantly fewer tears. The cold slows the enzyme reaction that releases the gas.

? Ask This Next

Why does food go bad? → #82

#82 Why Does Food Go Bad — And What's Growing on It?

Quick Answer

Food goes bad because bacteria and mold are everywhere. They land on food, multiply rapidly at room temperature, and break it down releasing waste products that smell and look unpleasant.

Let's Go Deeper

Bacteria can double in number every 20 minutes at room temperature. One bacterium becomes over a million in 7 hours. Mold spores are always in the air — they germinate when they land on moist food. Refrigeration slows bacterial growth by a factor of 10. Freezing stops it almost entirely. Salt, sugar and acid preserve food naturally.

Try It Yourself

Put two pieces of bread in separate bags — one dry, one with a few drops of water added. Seal both and leave for a week at room temperature. The damp bread molds much faster.

Ask This Next

Why does onion make you cry but not garlic? → #81

#83 Why Does Ice Cream Give You a Headache?

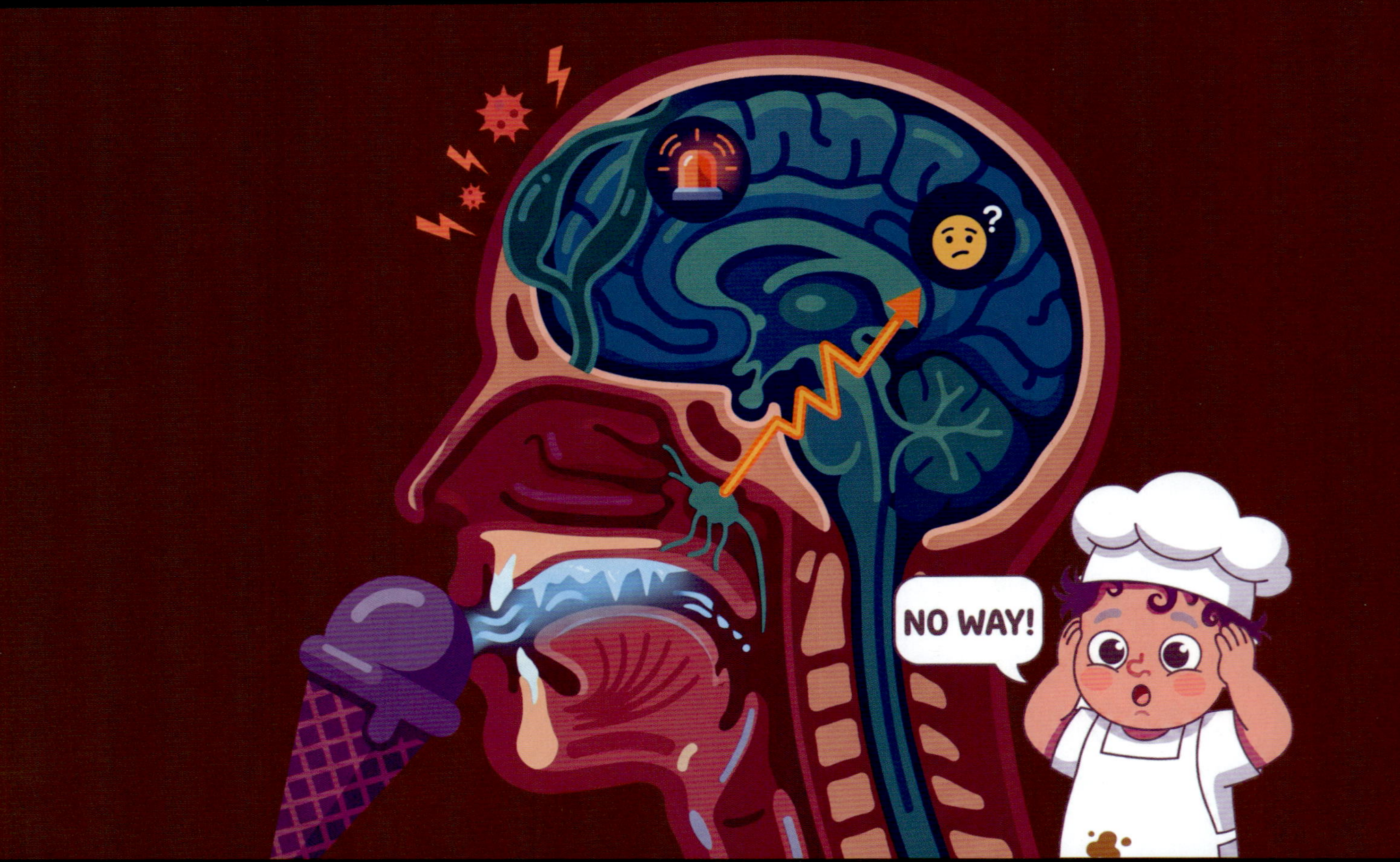

Quick Answer

Cold food chills the sphenopalatine ganglion — a nerve cluster behind your upper palate. Your brain misreads this as the whole head cooling and rapidly dilates blood vessels in the brain area.

Let's Go Deeper

The sphenopalatine ganglion is one of the largest nerve clusters in your head, close to the palate. It monitors brain temperature. When rapidly cooled it sends an emergency warming signal causing blood vessels to rapidly dilate — the same mechanism as a migraine. Pressing your tongue to the roof of your mouth warms it.

Try It Yourself

Next time you get brain freeze press your tongue firmly against the roof of your mouth. The warmth from your tongue transfers to the sphenopalatine ganglion reducing the pain.

Ask This Next

Why does chocolate make you feel happy?
→ #84

#84 Why Does Chocolate Make You Feel Happy?

Quick Answer

Chocolate triggers dopamine and serotonin release in your brain's reward system. It also contains phenylethylamine which produces feelings similar to being in love, and boosts mood naturally.

Let's Go Deeper

Chocolate is a complex chemical cocktail. Sugar and fat independently trigger the brain's pleasure reward system. Theobromine mildly stimulates the nervous system. Phenylethylamine is produced naturally when you fall in love. Serotonin precursors in chocolate may improve mood. The combination is uniquely psychologically rewarding.

Try It Yourself

Compare how you feel eating plain dark chocolate versus milk chocolate versus white chocolate. Dark has more theobromine and phenylethylamine. White has none because it lacks cocoa solids.

Ask This Next

Why do some farts smell worse? → #85

#85 Why Do Some Farts Smell So Much Worse?

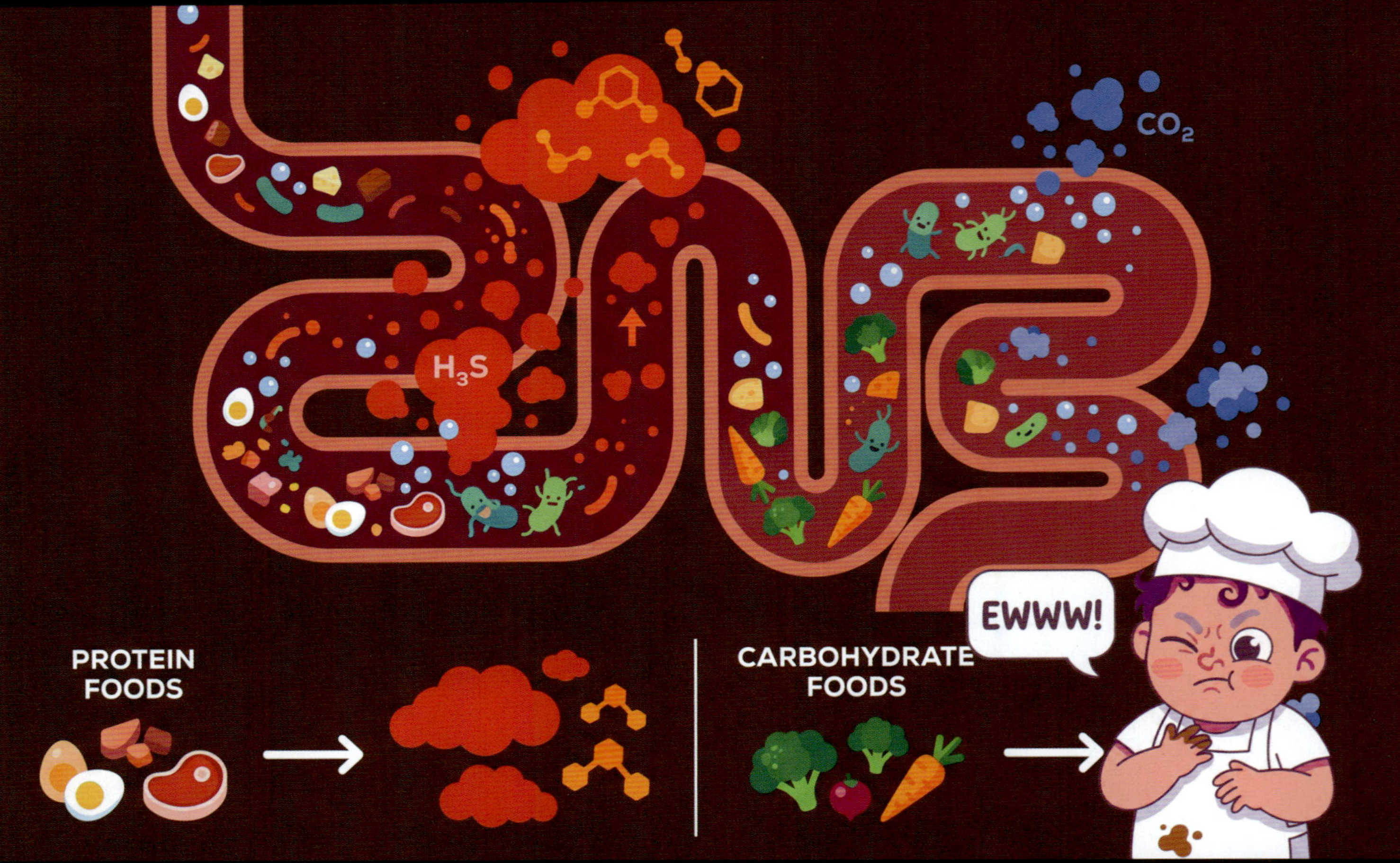

Quick Answer

The smell depends on what your gut bacteria are breaking down. Protein foods like meat and eggs produce sulfur compounds including hydrogen sulfide — the smell of rotten eggs.

Let's Go Deeper

About 99% of fart gas is odorless — nitrogen, oxygen, CO2, hydrogen and methane. Only 1% causes the smell but that 1% can be extremely potent. Sulfur-containing amino acids in protein foods are fermented by gut bacteria into sulfurous gases. Different gut bacteria populations produce different amounts — which is why smells vary.

Try It Yourself

Keep a two-day food diary alongside noting when you notice more or less gas and smell. Most people find a clear pattern — high protein days produce stronger sulfur odors.

? Ask This Next

Why does fizzy drink make you burp? → #86

#86 Why Does Fizzy Drink Make You Burp?

Quick Answer

Fizzy drinks are packed with CO2 gas dissolved under pressure. Once in your warm stomach the gas comes out of solution rapidly. Pressure builds until the lower esophageal sphincter opens.

Let's Go Deeper

CO2 is forced into drinks under high pressure — Henry's Law states that gas dissolves in liquid proportionally to pressure. When you open a bottle and drink it, the stomach's warmth and lower pressure cause rapid CO2 release. A 330ml can contains about 2.5 volumes of CO2 — more than double the drink's volume in gas form.

Try It Yourself

Shake a fizzy drink gently then open it slowly — lots of foam. Leave it undisturbed for 5 minutes then open again — much less foam. The shaking introduces tiny gas bubbles.

Ask This Next

Why does bread rise? → #76

Chapter 7

People & How We Work

Have you ever wondered why humans are the only animals that blush, why ancient Romans brushed their teeth with urine, or why you get butterflies in your stomach when you're nervous? In this chapter we explore 10 of the most fascinating questions about what makes humans uniquely, wonderfully and occasionally embarrassingly human.

In this chapter:

#87 Why Do Humans Laugh?

Quick Answer

Laughter is a social bonding signal that evolved before language. It releases endorphins that strengthen relationships, signals safety to others nearby, and is contagious because brains mirror emotions.

Let's Go Deeper

Humans laugh 30 times more often in social settings than alone. Laughter releases endorphins and oxytocin — bonding hormones. It signals to others that the situation is safe and playful. Chimps and rats also laugh during play — it is an ancient social tool. Most laughter is not a response to jokes but to social interaction.

Try It Yourself

Notice for one day when you laugh. Keep a tally of whether you are alone or with others each time. Research consistently shows people are 30 times more likely to laugh socially.

Ask This Next

Why do we cry? → #88

#88 Why Do We Cry?

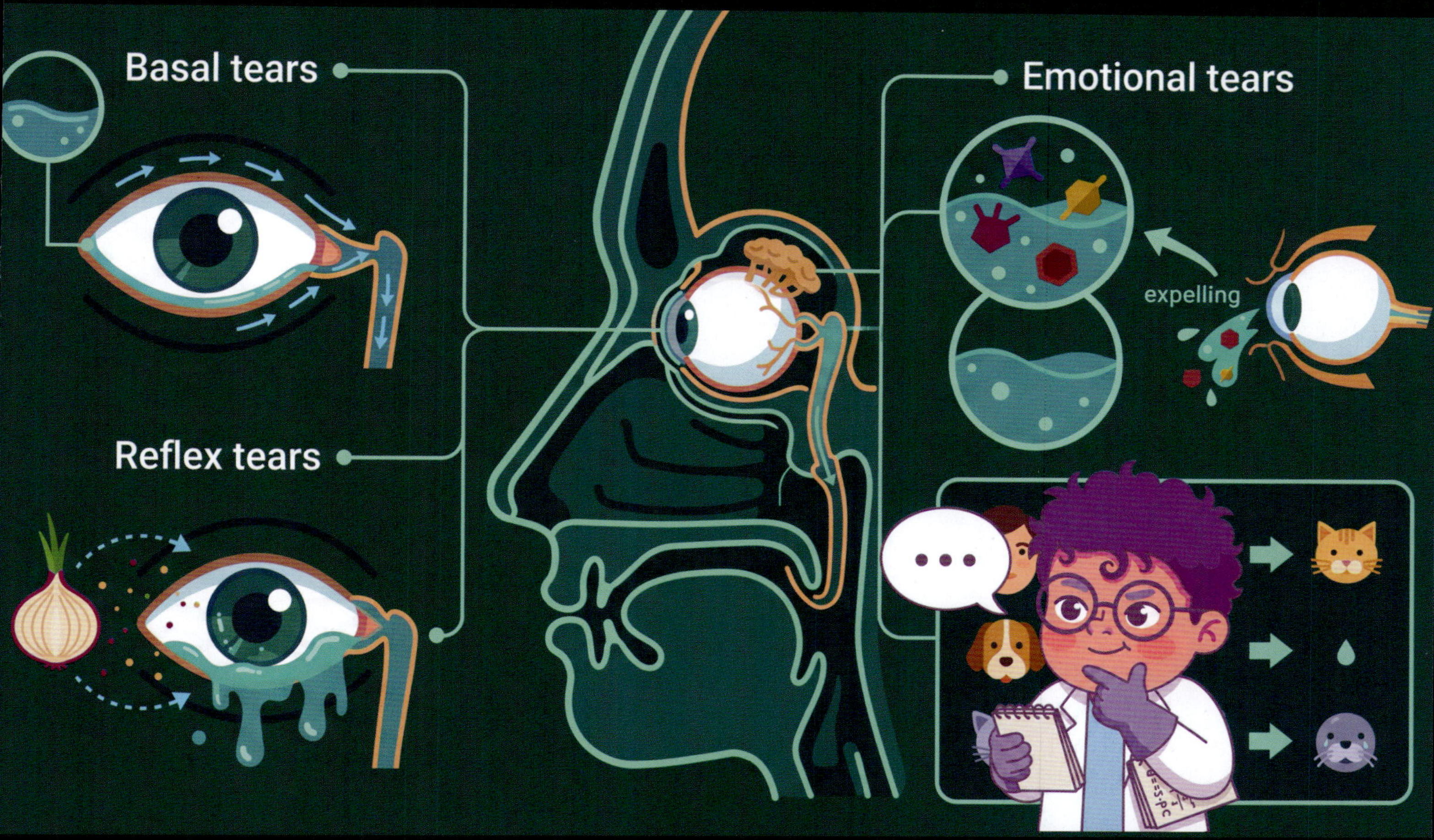

Quick Answer
Humans are the only animals that cry emotional tears. They contain stress hormones and endorphins — crying literally flushes stress chemicals from your body. It also signals a need for comfort.

Let's Go Deeper
There are three types of tears with different chemical compositions. Basal tears lubricate constantly. Reflex tears flush irritants. Emotional tears contain leucine enkephalin — a natural painkiller — and stress hormones including ACTH and prolactin. Crying releases these chemicals from the body explaining why people feel relieved.

Try It Yourself
Notice how you feel before and after a good cry. Most people report feeling calmer and less tense afterward — the stress hormone release and endorphin effect help regulate emotions.

Ask This Next
Why do humans laugh? → #87

#89 Why Do People Have Different Skin Colors?

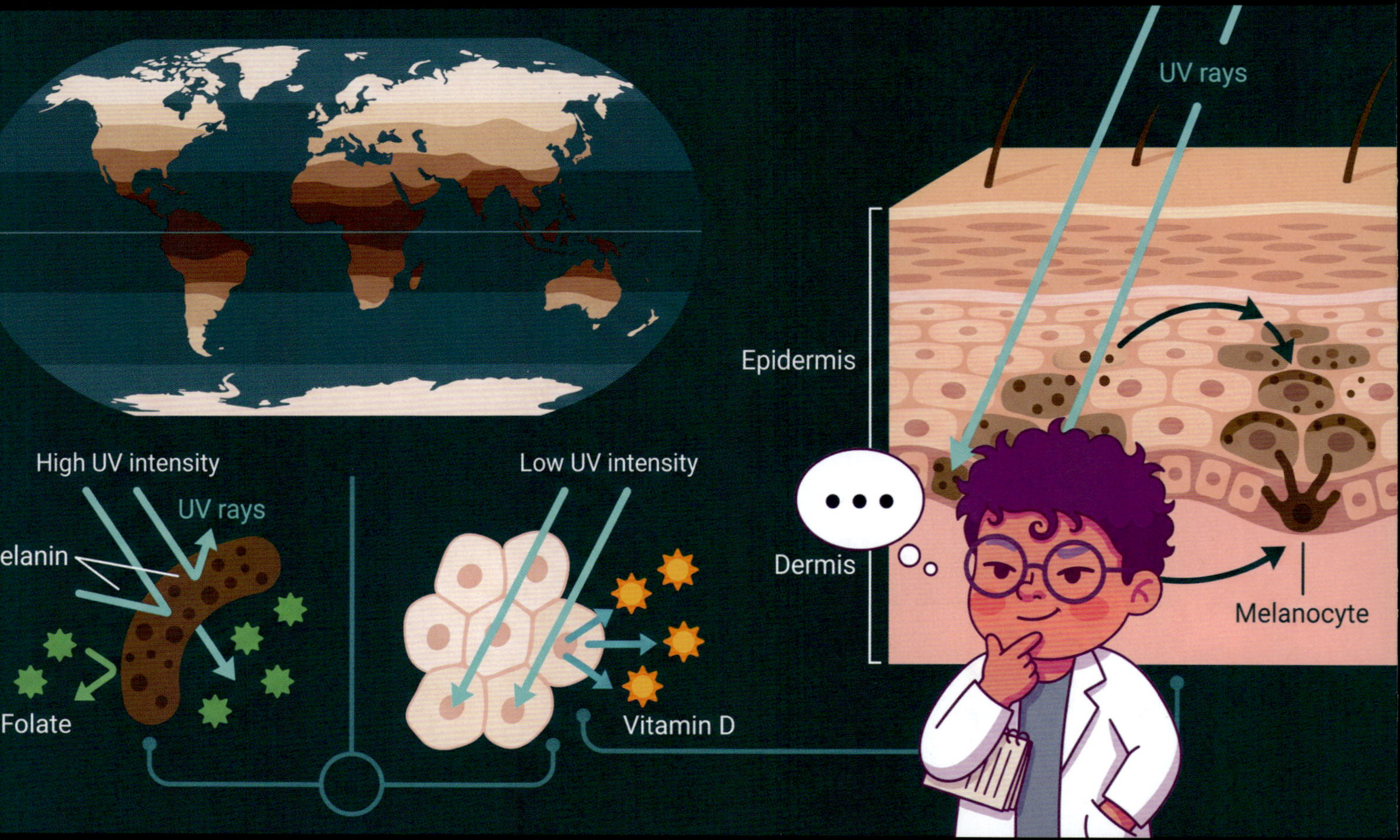

Quick Answer

Skin color is determined by melanin — a protective pigment. Near the equator where UV radiation is intense, more melanin protects against DNA damage. Further from the equator less melanin allows vitamin D production.

Let's Go Deeper

All humans have roughly the same number of melanocytes but different levels of melanin production. Dark skin evolved near the equator to protect folate — a vitamin essential for reproduction — from UV destruction. Light skin evolved at higher latitudes where weaker sunlight required less melanin blocking to absorb more UV.

Try It Yourself

Use UV-sensitive beads — they turn purple in sunlight. Take them inside under artificial light — they stay clear. The UV intensity difference between indoors and sunlight is massive.

Ask This Next

Why do humans have names? → #94

#90 Why Did Humans Start Cooking Food?

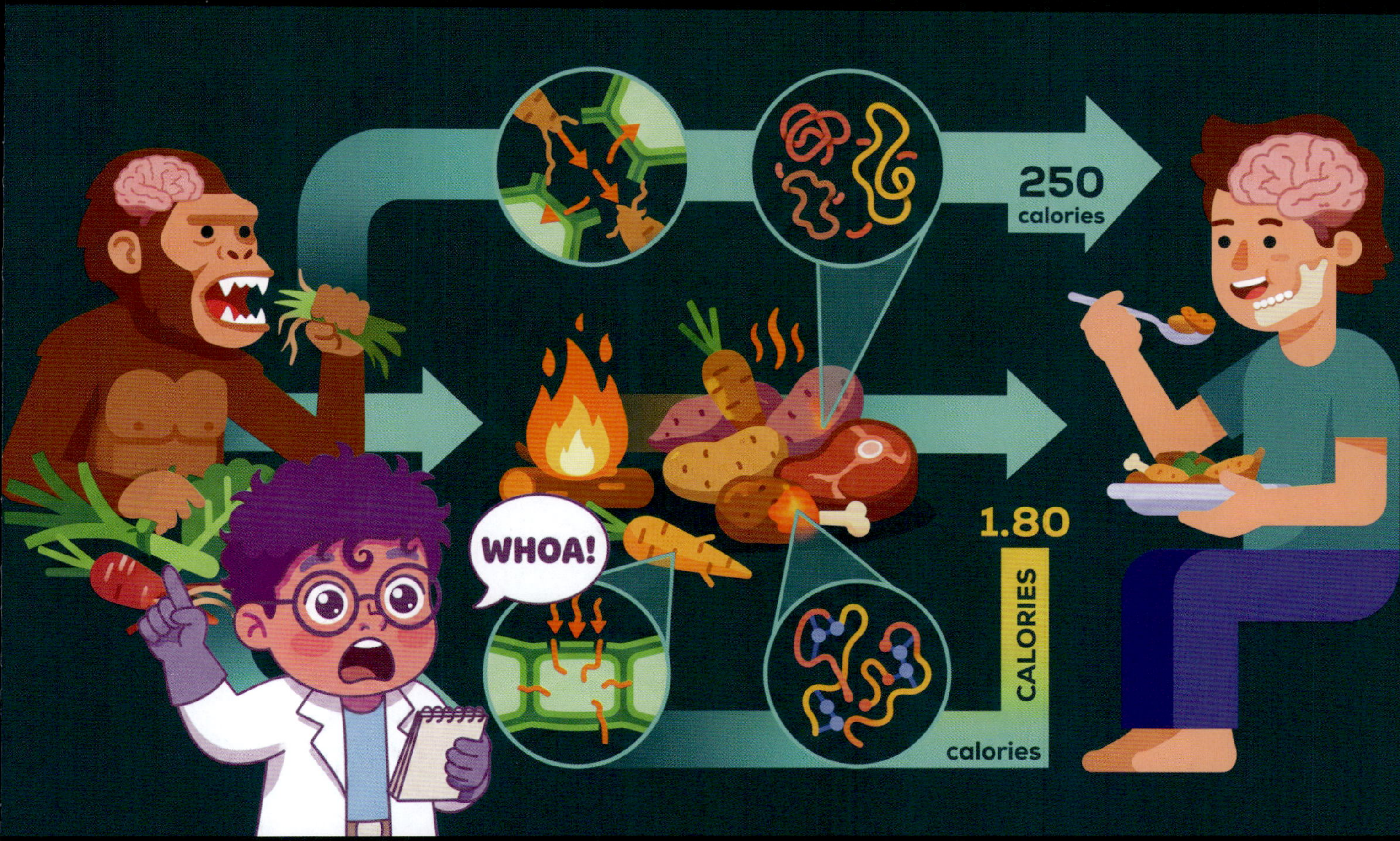

Quick Answer

Cooking unlocks far more calories from food by breaking down tough fibers and proteins before digestion. This calorie windfall allowed our brains to grow larger — our big brains require enormous energy.

Let's Go Deeper

Richard Wrangham's cooking hypothesis proposes that cooking was the key turning point in human evolution. A raw food diet requires 6-8 hours of chewing per day. Cooking pre-digests food externally releasing up to 40% more calories from the same amount of food. The freed energy fueled brain growth over millions of years.

Try It Yourself

Compare chewing time for a raw carrot versus a cooked carrot. The raw one requires many more chews and feels less satisfying despite being identical food.

Ask This Next

Why do people have different skin colors?
→ #89

#91 Why Do Humans Have So Many Languages?

Quick Answer

Languages diverge when groups of people separate and stop communicating. Small changes accumulate over generations until the two groups can no longer understand each other. There is no fixed endpoint.

Let's Go Deeper

All humans descended from small African populations that spread across the world. Geographic isolation — mountains, oceans, distance — separated groups whose languages then changed independently. Languages change at roughly 10-15% per thousand years. After 1,500 years of separation two related languages may become unintelligible.

Try It Yourself

Play telephone with a group — whisper a sentence through 10 people. Hear how it changes. Now imagine that process over thousands of years across millions of daily conversations.

Ask This Next

Why did humans start cooking food? → #90

#92 Why Do Humans Live So Much Longer Than Animals?

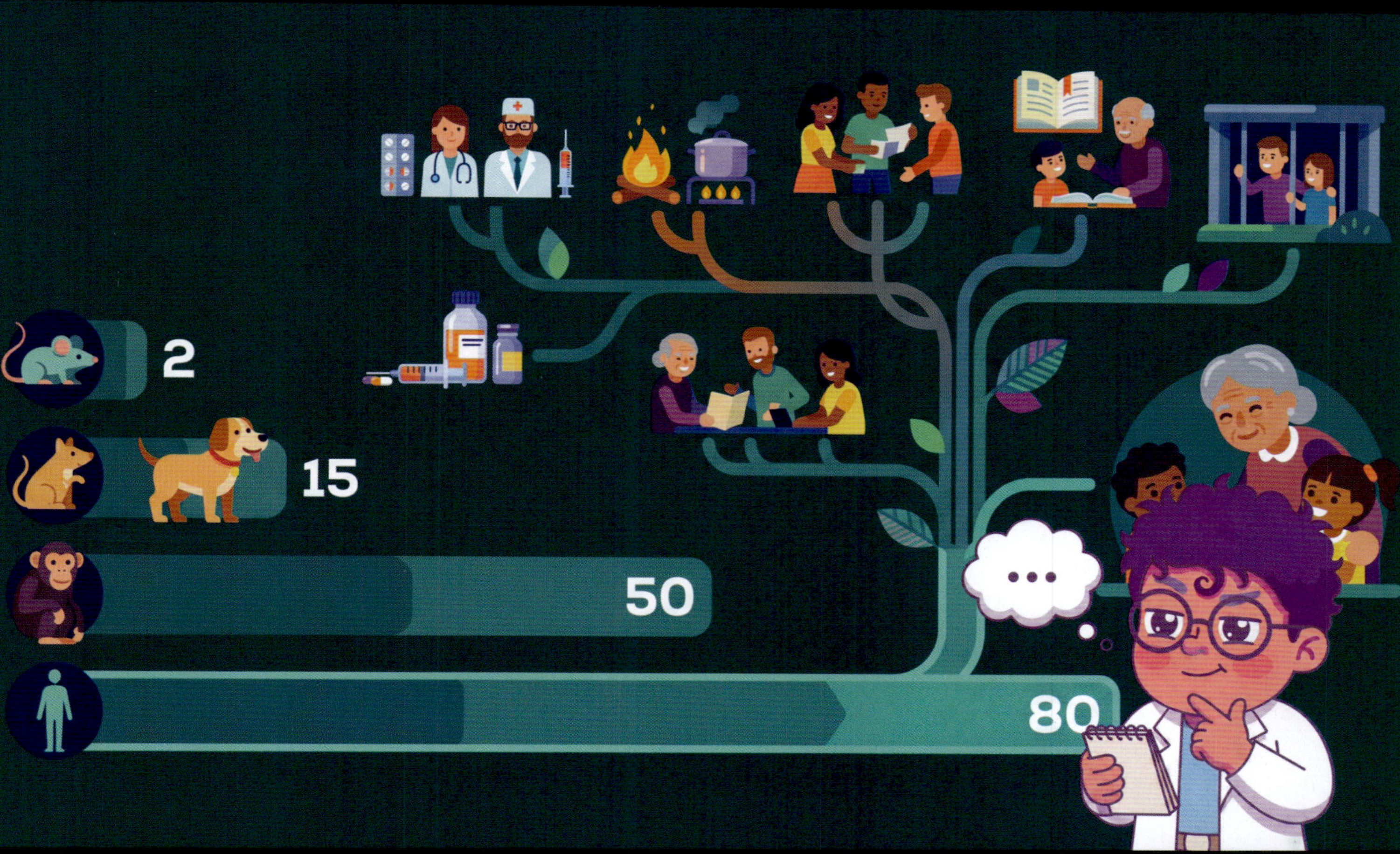

⚡ Quick Answer

Humans live long because we cook food, use medicine, cooperate socially, and pass knowledge across generations. Long-lived grandparents also help raise grandchildren improving survival rates.

Let's Go Deeper

Lifespan correlates strongly with brain size — bigger brains need more time to develop and learn. Human children are dependent far longer than any other animal. The grandmother hypothesis proposes that post-reproductive women increase grandchild survival enough to be evolutionarily advantageous. Medicine and social cooperation extend lifespan further.

Try It Yourself

Research the oldest living animal species. The Greenland shark lives over 400 years, some clams reach 500 years. These animals have extremely slow metabolisms.

? Ask This Next

Why do humans have so many languages? → #91

#93 Why Do We Get Butterflies in Our Stomach?

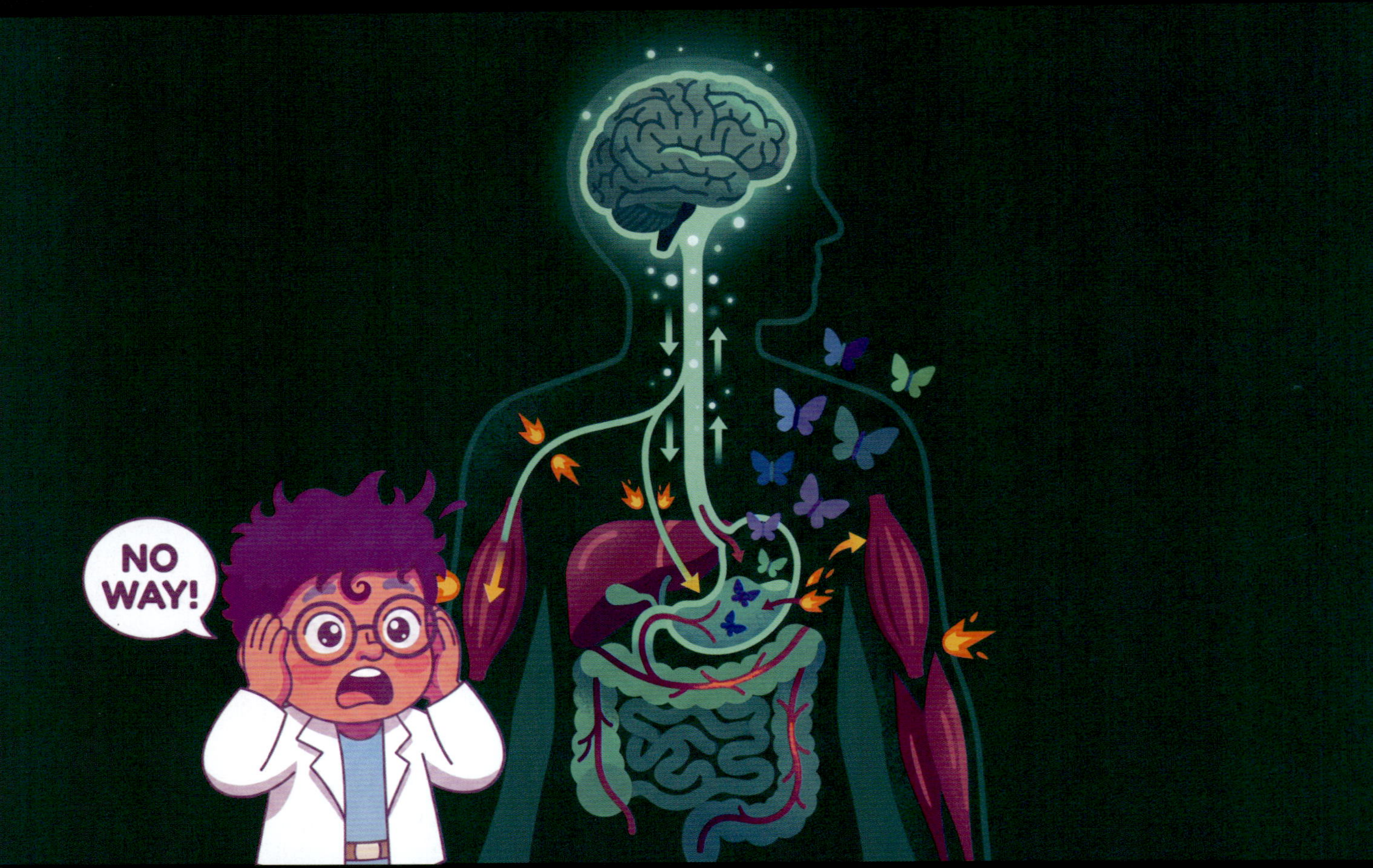

Quick Answer

When anxious your body releases adrenaline which diverts blood away from your digestive system to your muscles. The reduced blood flow causes the fluttery sensation in your stomach.

Let's Go Deeper

Your gut contains 500 million neurons — more than your spinal cord — connected to your brain via the vagus nerve. This gut-brain axis sends signals both ways. Stress signals cause the digestive system to slow down as the body prioritizes fight-or-flight. The gut has its own nervous system that continues working independently.

Try It Yourself

Before something that makes you nervous notice your stomach feeling. Now try slow deep breathing — 4 seconds in, 4 seconds hold, 6 seconds out. Notice how the fluttering decreases.

Ask This Next

Why do humans live so much longer than animals? → #92

#94 Why Do Humans Have Names?

⚡ Quick Answer

Names evolved because humans live in large social groups too big to track by face alone. Names allow us to talk about specific absent people, coordinate complex cooperation, and maintain social bonds.

Let's Go Deeper

Chimps live in groups of about 20 and recognise each other by face and smell — no names needed. Humans regularly manage social networks of 150 or more people — Dunbar's number. Names allow reference to absent individuals, enable complex planning and allow reputation to travel. Surnames emerged as villages grew into cities.

Try It Yourself

Try to describe a specific person to someone without using their name or pointing at them. Notice how difficult it becomes — you need extensive description of their appearance and traits.

? Ask This Next

Why do we get butterflies in our stomach? → #93

#95 Why Did Romans Brush Their Teeth With Urine?

⚡ Quick Answer

Urine contains ammonia — a powerful natural cleaning agent. Romans discovered it whitened teeth and killed bacteria effectively. It actually worked. Modern toothpaste still uses related compounds.

Let's Go Deeper

Urine was so valued as a cleaning agent in ancient Rome that it was collected and taxed by Emperor Vespasian — leading to the saying pecunia non olet — money does not smell. Ammonia from urine was used for laundry, tanning leather and teeth cleaning. Portuguese sailors from the 1600s reportedly used it too.

Try It Yourself

Mix a small amount of baking soda with water and brush your teeth with it. Baking soda is also alkaline — the same chemistry principle the Romans used with ammonia cleaners.

❓ Ask This Next

Why are humans the only animals that blush? → #96

#96 Why Are Humans the Only Animals That Blush?

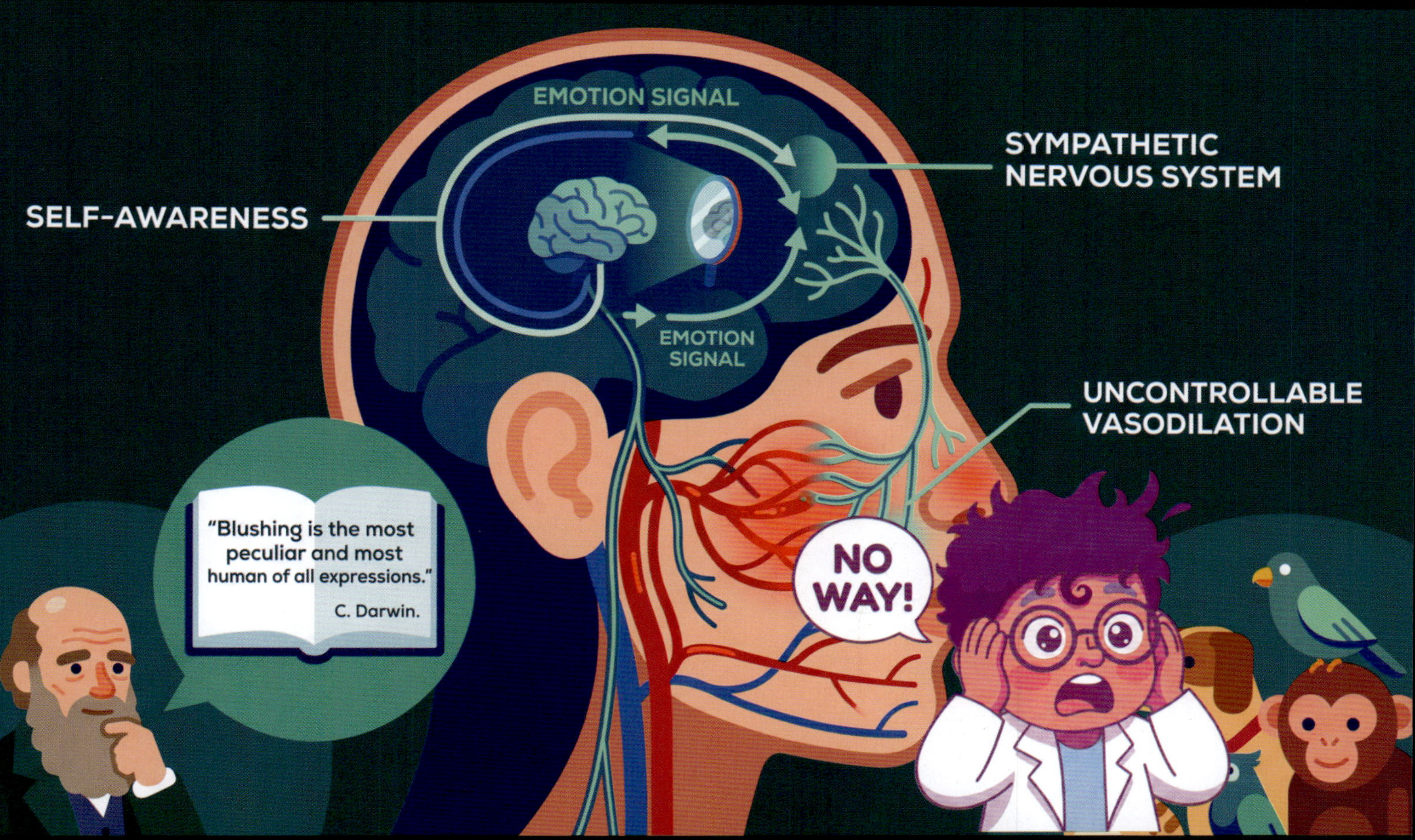

⚡ Quick Answer

Blushing requires self-awareness — knowing that others are watching and judging you. Only humans have this level of social self-consciousness. The blush itself is an involuntary stress response.

Let's Go Deeper

Darwin called blushing the most peculiar and most human of all expressions. It is triggered by the sympathetic nervous system but cannot be consciously controlled — you cannot blush on command or stop a blush once started. It requires theory of mind — the ability to imagine what others think of you. No other animal shows true blushing.

Try It Yourself

Try to blush deliberately right now. You cannot. Now remember a genuinely embarrassing moment in detail — you probably feel warmth in your face. The blush is completely involuntary.

? Ask This Next

Why do humans laugh? → #87

Chapter 8

Big Questions

Some questions don't have complete answers yet. Scientists are still working on them. In this final chapter we explore 5 of the biggest questions humans have ever asked — about life, death, dinosaurs, water and the universe itself. These are the questions that keep scientists up at night. Now they can keep you up too.

In this chapter:

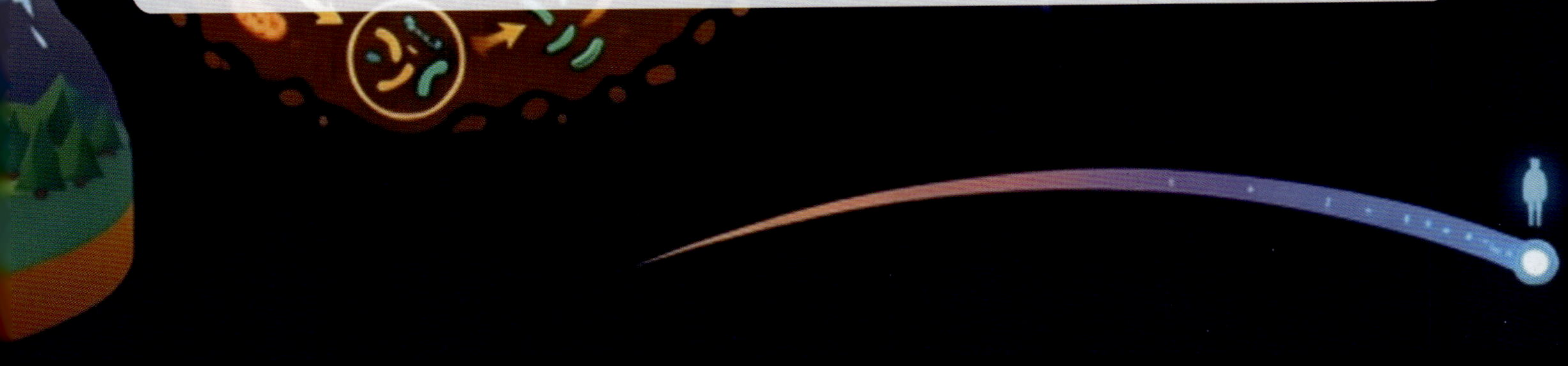

#97 Why Might There Be Life on Other Planets?

Quick Answer

There are more stars in the universe than grains of sand on all Earth's beaches. Many have planets. Life on Earth exists in boiling vents and frozen ice. The odds that we are completely alone are tiny.

Let's Go Deeper

The Milky Way alone contains 200-400 billion stars. NASA estimates there are more potentially habitable planets in our galaxy than there are people on Earth. We have found life thriving in conditions once thought impossible — near volcanic vents, in acidic lakes, in frozen Antarctic rock. Life appears to be extremely adaptable.

Try It Yourself

Look up the nearest star to our sun — Proxima Centauri, 4.2 light years away. At the speed of our fastest spacecraft it would take about 75,000 years to reach our nearest neighbor.

Ask This Next

Why did the dinosaurs really disappear? → #98

#98 Why Did the Dinosaurs Really Disappear?

Quick Answer

A 10km asteroid struck Mexico 66 million years ago releasing energy equivalent to a billion nuclear bombs. The impact winter that followed — dust blocking sunlight for years — collapsed global ecosystems.

Let's Go Deeper

The Chicxulub impact struck the Yucatán Peninsula with the force of 10 billion Hiroshima bombs. The immediate blast and tsunamis were catastrophic but the real killer was the impact winter — dust and sulfur aerosols blocked sunlight for years, collapsing photosynthesis. Dinosaurs that couldn't adapt eventually died out.

Try It Yourself

Find the Chicxulub crater on Google Maps — it is still visible as a semicircular bay off Mexico's Yucatán coast 66 million years later. The crater is 180km wide.

Ask This Next

Why are we the only animals that talk? → #99

#99 Why Are We the Only Animals That Talk?

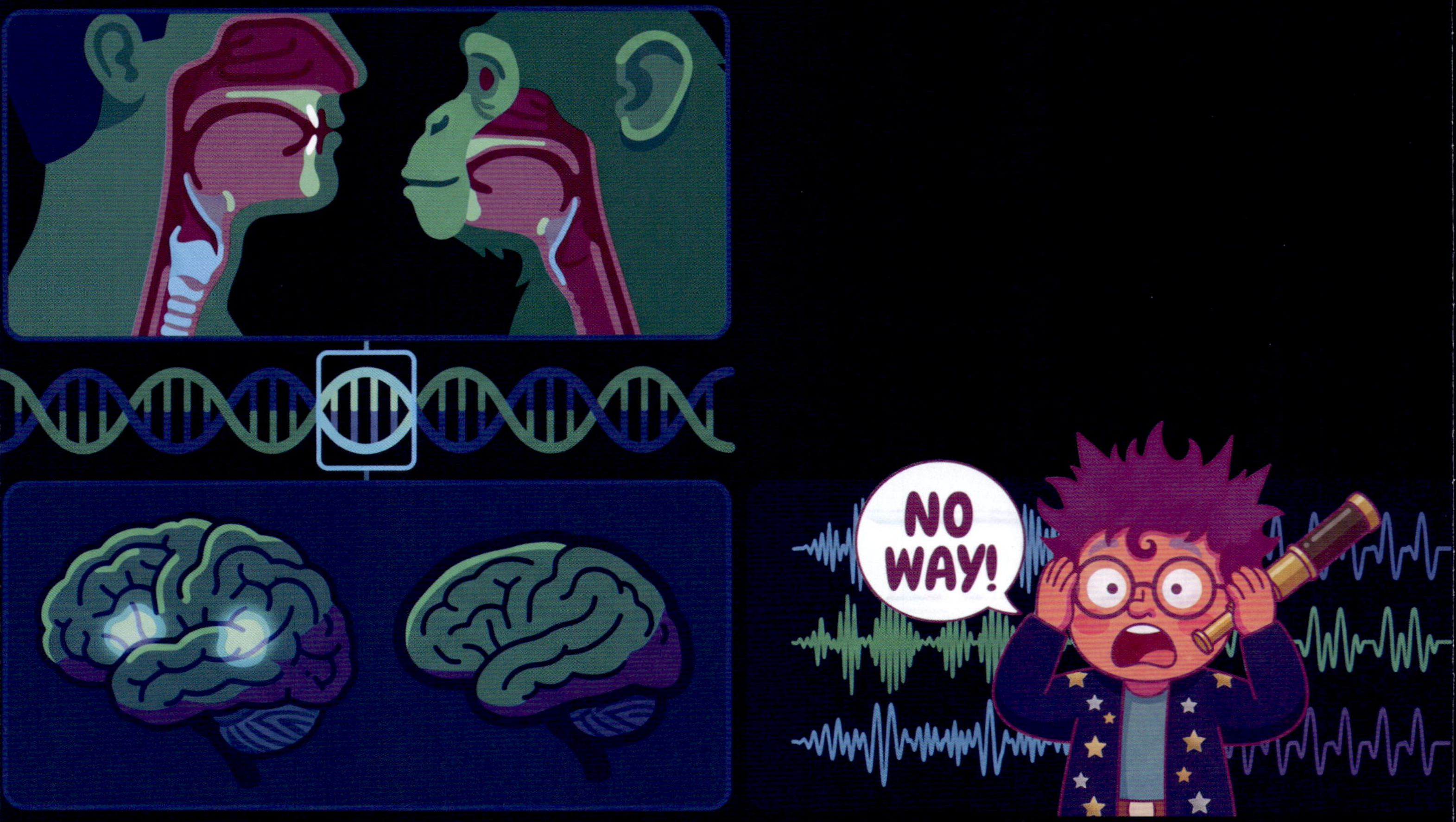

⚡ Quick Answer

Humans have a uniquely descended larynx, a specialized FOXP2 gene, and dedicated brain regions for language — Broca's area and Wernicke's area. No other animal has all three. We still do not fully understand language evolution.

Let's Go Deeper

The human larynx sits lower in the throat than in any other primate — allowing a wider range of sounds but making choking a genuine risk. The FOXP2 gene is associated with fine motor control of the mouth and throat. Neanderthals had a similar version of FOXP2 suggesting they may have had some speech capabilities too.

Try It Yourself

Try to make the full range of vowel sounds — ah, ee, oo, oh, uh. Now try to make them while keeping your tongue completely flat and still. Impossible. The fine tongue movements shape speech.

? Ask This Next

Will we ever run out of water? → #100

#100 Will We Ever Run Out of Water?

Quick Answer

Earth will never lose its water — it just recycles. But freshwater distribution is shifting. The same amount of water now serves 8 billion people. Droughts and shifting rainfall create water shortages.

Let's Go Deeper

97.5% of Earth's water is saltwater. Of the 2.5% freshwater, 69% is locked in glaciers and ice caps. Only about 0.3% of all Earth's water is accessible surface freshwater in rivers and lakes. Climate change is not reducing total water — it is concentrating rainfall in some areas while creating permanent drought in others.

Try It Yourself

Audit your own water use for one day — drinking, washing, toilet flushing, food production. The average person in a developed country uses about 150 litres per day directly.

Ask This Next

What happens to your body after you die?
→ #101

#101 What Happens to Your Body After You Die?

Quick Answer

Your atoms do not disappear — they return to the world and become part of other living things. The carbon, oxygen and nitrogen that make you today were once part of stars, ancient oceans and organisms.

Let's Go Deeper

Within hours after death bacteria that lived in your gut begin breaking down your body from the inside. Over weeks and months decomposers return your atoms to the soil. Those atoms are then taken up by plants, eaten by animals and cycled through countless living things. Every atom in your body has been part of something else before.

Try It Yourself

Start a compost bin with food scraps, leaves and garden waste. Observe it over several weeks — the material transforms from recognizable objects into dark rich soil-like compost.

Ask This Next

Why might there be life on other planets? → #97

Thank You!

Thanks a Bunch for Reading!

I'm really glad you picked up this book—and I hope it gave you and your child something useful, whether it was a family bonding moment, engaged questions from your kids or just a few "I didn't know that!" moments. I enjoyed creating it as well, especially as a mum of young kids.

If you enjoyed it, I'd be super grateful if you could take a minute to leave a quick review online. Your feedback helps other readers know what to expect, and it means a lot to me personally, too. In return, I promise to read every single review and take in the feedback to make better books for you.

Thanks again for being part of this. Your support for me as a small independent author seriously makes a huge difference!

Cheers,

Claire Monroe
ChangeLifeReads